A
Busy Person's Guide
to a Life You Love

*9 Quick and Easy Ways to Create and Find Time
to Enjoy Your Best Possible Life*

Jamie Novak

Contact Virtualbookworm.com to order books.
877-376-4955
PO Box 9949, College Station, TX 77842

Edited by Robin Quinn
Interior illustrations and layout by Gale Sisul

"A Busy Person's Guide to a Life You Love." ISBN 1-58939-292-2.

Library of Congress Control Number: 2002117131

Published 2002 by Virtualbookworm.com Publishing Inc., P.O. Box 9949, College Station, TX , 77842, US. ©2002 Jamie Novak. All rights reserved. No part of this publication may be reproduced, stored in a retrieval system, or transmitted in any form or by any means, electronic, mechanical, recording or otherwise, without the prior written permission of Jamie Novak.

Manufactured in the United States of America

Number 1 in the Life U Love Series

Dedication

To busy people everywhere

Acknowledgements

The following people have added something extraordinary to my life. I wish to thank each of them by acknowledging them now. First and foremost there's my husband, José, who let me squeeze in "just one more page" night after night before we spent time together. His support of me is never ending, his belief in me is unwavering, and his faith in me means the world. I would also like to thank my parents, Jim and Sue, who are always there for me and who instilled in me a real love of books. Thanks also goes to my sisters, Brandy, Jessica and Kristy, who always like what I write no matter what. Kudos to my faithful dog, Romeo, who listened to many rough drafts and thought each one was great. I am grateful to John and Lee Coffey who thought every idea I ever had was a good one. Your support means a lot to me and I have enjoyed every dinner we have ever shared. Thanks as well to Bob Coffey who extended a very generous offer to contact him any time with questions. He is a wealth of knowledge and a great guy. I would like to acknowledge Deb Giffen, my coach, for helping me realize things about myself I had never known. I am indebted to Gale Sisul for laying out this book in a reader friendly way, for the icons that appear throughout the book, and for my fabulous website. You are always just a click away to help me solve my computer issues. Gale, you're a true gem. Thanks to my editor, Robin Quinn, who made my ideas come to life on every page. She is the best editor anyone could hope to work with. I am grateful to Bobby Bernshausen and Virtualbookworm.com. I could not have done this without them. They are so patient and explained everything, sometimes more than once. I must thank Mrs. Gail Williams, my middle-school English teacher, who taught me about creative writing. I also must acknowledge Ms. Sandra Kling, my favorite teacher, who taught me about raising my self-esteem and helped me to build confidence in myself during my formative years. I am indebted to Eben Lowenthal for helping me along in my journey to find a life that I love. And finally I would like to thank Pat Thompson who listened to my idea for this book and said I should be the one to write it.

Interior layout and website design:
Webpage Designs by Gale
Gale Sisul
www.webpagedesignsbygale.com
gsisul@csonline.net

Author photo:
Image Shots
Linda Kim
255 Woodbridge Center
Woodbridge, NJ 07095
(732) 326-1034

Author make-up:
Clinique at Lord & Taylor
Joy Galucci
250 Woodbridge Center
Woodbridge, NJ 07095
(732) 750-3232

Editing services:
Quinn's Word for Word
Robin Quinn
QuinnRobin@aol.com

Author hairstyle:
Hair Cuttery
Heather Hartwig
Blue Star Shopping Center
1701-10 Route 22 West
Watchung, NJ 7060
(908) 322-9742

Table of Contents

Chapter 3: Now learn to say "no" gracefully while getting everything else you need done.
AKA Managing Your Time and Priorities

Chapter 4: After that, start putting yourself first, without neglecting anyone else. AKA Self care and nurturing

Chapter 8: Next figure out what you want and how to get it. AKA Reaching for Your Dreams and Goals

Chapter 9: After that, do everything but move into a log cabin with no running water. AKA Simplifying and Getting Down to the Basics

Chapter 10: Now tie it up in a nice, neat package.
AKA Pulling It All Together

Appendix

Index

Introduction

Something about this book caught your eye. What was it? Was it the idea of living a life you love instead of one packed full of things you feel you have to do and short on time to do them in? Or maybe you thought of simplifying your life or having time for yourself. Maybe it was the idea of finally getting organized or clearing out your clutter once and for all. Or are you looking for ways to lessen your stress or to find your true passion? Whether it's just to clear off your dining room table, to locate a job you love, or to write the great American novel -- whatever your desire is -- the answer lies inside. Come take a journey with me through nine easy-to-master, hard-to-forget ways of bringing more balance and joy into your life. It's all about you creating and having time to enjoy a life you love.

Before we begin, let me tell you a little about how I came to write this book. The short and sweet version is that one day I just decided I was going to start living a life I loved, no matter what anyone else thought or said about me. But it is *how* I came to this decision that is the real story.

You see I was an expert people pleaser; know anyone like that? I could anticipate your needs before you knew them yourself, and I was there to help in any way, shape or form I could -- no matter what it cost me personally. It gave me a sense of self-worth and satisfaction to be able to help someone else. I was constantly on the go, never still long enough to think about anything but the next thing I had to do. I was busy, but always willing to take on more. I put others' needs ahead of mine; in fact, I was not even sure what my needs were! I did everything perfectly and I was convinced the world could not run without me. What I didn't realize was that I was actually hurting myself and at the same time taking away other people's ability to do things for themselves.

I was the one everyone could depend on and I'll admit it was nice to be needed. But slowly I started to feel a sense of dissatisfaction creeping in. At first, I was not exactly sure what I was dissatisfied with. But after months of this nagging feeling lingering, I thought it was time to take a closer look. I decided to spend some time evaluating my life.

I looked at all areas. First I spoke with a therapist to try to gain some perspective. Then I thought I might be dissatisfied with my job, so I sought out a career counselor. I thought I might be struggling financially, so I sat down with a financial analyst. I read a bookshelf full of self-improvement books, but still that nagging feeling stuck with me. What could this be? I thought.

As a last resort, I took some advice and started a journal. I journaled when I woke up each morning and before I went to bed each night. Still nothing! However I persisted, and sure enough, after about a week, I started to see some patterns developing. I found myself complaining about the state of my life. I complained that I had to help my friend find an apartment and that I promised to pet sit for another friend. I complained that I had committed to cover shifts for a co-worker and that I was lending money when I did not have any extra to lend.

Finally I came to the conclusion that I resented sacrificing my time, money and energy. I realized that I alone am responsible for how I spend my time, money and energy on a daily basis. If I did not feel happy with how I was spending it, then it was my choice to do things differently. After all, life is full of choices; all I had to do was make different ones.

"Only I can change my life. No one can do it for me." Carol Burnett

I was overstressed, overworked and just plain tired. I wished that I could stop the world and jump off. That's when I held up the big, red stop sign and yelled, what about me? This is my life! Enough, it's time for me! I realized then I could stop being tired of being sick and tired, and you can too.

Here are some things I have learned to stop doing:

➢ Stopped trying to please everyone
➢ Stopped trying to be liked by everyone
➢ Stopped trying to be the star at the expense of my own life
➢ Stopped trying to do everything perfectly
➢ Stopped trying to do everything

"If you always do what you've always done, you always get what you've always got. To change our output, we must change our input." Author Unknown

I started a group where all of us people pleasers, can't say no'ers, over-committed, underappreciated, generally dissatisfied, busy worrywarts of the world could meet and talk about ways to improve the quality of our lives. We discussed ways to simplify, how to keep track of our time, and ways to better manage our commitments. We spoke about caring for ourselves, nurturing ourselves, and taking time to do the things *we* want to -- without feeling guilty. We even talked about clearing clutter and managing a household. We thought of clever ways to balance work with life. Our talks even went into managing finances and setting priorities. We shared goals and dreams for our future and celebrated when we reached them. People's goals ranged from taking five minutes out for themselves, to changing careers, to fulfilling their passion in life.

What I came to find out was that I wasn't the only one struggling with these issues. There were lots of us out there expending our energy on the wrong things hoping for happiness and fulfillment. What we learned as a group is that true happiness and fulfillment comes from the inside.

So I blended my inborn organizational skills, my newfound knowledge, my desire to help others, and my passion for writing, and out came my company, A Life U Love along with this book. That's how my book came to be. So with that being said, let's set out on our journey to help you create a life that you love while finding time for you to enjoy it.

How to Use This Book

If you want to lead a life you love living, this book is going to show you how. You have actually already taken the first step! The first step was to decide that you're ready to make some changes. You've made up your heart and mind. Step One is out of the way. Now it's time to look at how you can stop wasting time on unimportant things so that you can spend more time on the things that *do* matter to you.

Remember that it has taken a number of years to create the life you have. There are no overnight fixes. Sorry! However, by working on the steps outlined in this book, you'll start seeing results within the next twenty-eight days. <u>Be patient and give yourself time.</u> <u>The changes will come.</u>

It takes twenty-eight days to create a new habit. You have to actually do something new twenty-eight times before it becomes second nature. So give yourself time. Don't expect overnight changes.

Begin by questioning and evaluating everything you do for the next month. And I mean *everything*. From where you keep the toothpaste, to who should open your mail at work, to who you offer to help. Ask yourself, is there a better way, a quicker way, or a simpler way of doing this? Ponder if it needs to be done at all, and if so, are you the one who should be doing it? You're going to challenge yourself so you can make some adjustments. In some areas you may do more in other cases do less, and in most cases you'll just do it differently.

You may have heard this story before, but it bears repeating. A husband watched as his newlywed wife prepared a roast for cooking. He asked, "Why do you cut off the ends?" She replied, "I don't know. That's how my mother does it." So the next time the young man saw his mother-in-law, he asked her, "When you are preparing a roast, why do you cut off the ends?" She replied, "I don't know. That's how my mother always does it." Curious now, the mother-in-law decided to call her mother. She asked, "Mom, when you're preparing a roast, why do you cut off the ends?" Her mother replied, "Because that's the only way to make it fit in my roasting pan."

Ask yourself, are you doing things your way or someone else's?

You're currently following the pattern that your life has been in for some time. This is now an opportunity to shake things up and reevaluate how you're using your time and energy. I was once working with someone who constantly complained that she never got to complete a task. She would start something and never finish for one of a variety of reasons. But when she stepped back and took a look at why, she was then able to make a simple change that allowed her to complete tasks start to finish. This not only allowed her to get more done by at the end of the day, she had a sense of accomplishment. Her self-worth grew as her list of tasks to do diminished.

This is exactly what I'm talking about. Examine your life for the next twenty-eight days to see what can be adjusted so you can start living a life you love instead of simply going with the flow. Your routine is not satisfying to you anymore.

There's a lot of information in the pages of this book and it can feel overwhelming. You're going to pick what you like and try it. You are not going to change everything. Instead, make small, simple changes that have the power to transform your life.

"It's not so much that we're afraid of change or so in love with the old ways, but it's that place in between that

we fear . . . . It's like being between trapezes. It's Linus when his blanket is in the dryer." Marilyn Ferguson

"Change your thoughts and you change your world." Norman Vincent Peale

This is your book so write in the margins, highlight passages and stick Post Its all over it. As you read, make notes about what strikes a cord with you. This book is a continued resource to be used over and over again.

Throughout the book you'll see the following icons. Each one highlights a different portion of text in order to draw your attention to that section.

Icon Key

Tip/Trick		Caution	
Story		Bright Idea	
Key		Time/money/ sanity saver	
Minute Muncher		Statistic	
Quote			

First you have to stop muttering, "I know it's here somewhere!"
AKA Clutter Control

This section is for you if:

- ➢ You toss stuff into bags and hide them when you hear company is coming over.
- ➢ You have stacks of stuff around and cannot see the top of your dining room table.
- ➢ You have one or more drawers known as "junk drawers."
- ➢ You have a drawer that will not close unless you push stuff down.
- ➢ Stuff falls out of your closet when you open it.

Or if any of this sounds like something you would be likely to say:

- ➢ I want to get organized but I just don't know where to begin.
- ➢ If I had more room, all my storage problems would be solved.
- ➢ I often misplace my glasses and/or car keys.
- ➢ It's hard for me to decide what to throw away.

Introduction-

Clutter. We all have it but what exactly is it? Clutter is stuff that collects and does not have a home. It's often the result of having too much stuff. In getting rid of clutter, a good initial question is how much stuff is enough? Do you really need three pairs of black shoes? Or a drawerful of plastic shopping bags? Or subscriptions to all six magazines? Better that you should have a few things that you love and use than so much stuff that you don't really know what you have. Also remember, you can't put something away if you don't know where it goes. And let's be honest; chances are you will only put it away if it's easy to do. So everything has to have a place to go when it's not in use.

Here are some common thoughts that instantly lead to clutter:

> I should keep it. One day I might need it.
> I'll get to it tomorrow.
> I'll finish it up later.
> No one can make me clean up if I don't feel like it.
> Later I'll have the time to organize everything perfectly.
> Oh, I have to keep this. It reminds me of….

Any of these sound familiar? If so, change your way of thinking. Here are some examples:

Old thought:	I should keep it. One day I might need it.
New thought:	If I ever need something like this again, I can get one.
Old thought:	I'll get to it tomorrow.
New thought:	Develop a "do it now" attitude.
Old thought:	I'll finish it up later.
New thought:	I'll put it away partially done and pull it out again when I have time to finish it.

Old thought:	No one can make me clean up if I don't feel like it.
New thought:	True, but come on you're a grown-up now.

Old thought:	Later I'll have the time to organize everything perfectly.
New thought:	There's no such thing as perfect and time does not just suddenly appear. Schedule time to do it and do a good job. You can always touch it up later.

Old thought:	Oh, I have to keep this. It reminds me of….
New thought:	Keep one or two special mementoes of the occasion and get rid of the rest. Memories are in your mind not in objects.

5 Keys for beating clutter

There are five keys to conquering clutter for good. They are:

#1

Keep "Like Things" Together.

This key saves you time, energy, money and your sanity. It saves you money because if you can find the one you have, you won't need to buy a duplicate. Key #1 saves you time and energy because you don't have to hunt around for items. Imagine all your work clothes together on one side of the closet ready to wear, all your bills together ready to be paid, and all of your kids' toys picked up and put away. All "like things" should be stored together.

 Clutter creates 40% more housework.

#2

One in, One out.

Remember that the less you have, the less you have to worry about. So before you bring something new into your

3

house, ask yourself, "Do I really need this?" If so, then ask, "Do I have a place to put it?" If so, then go ahead and get it. But stick to the One in, One Out Rule. When you bring something new into the house, toss out something old. For example: If you buy a new skirt, hang the new one up on the hanger of the old one. Tossing the old one out or give it away.

Just because it's free doesn't mean you have to get it.

It's that easy; simply remember "One in, One out." Hold free items to the same standard as things you would buy. I know people who have drawers full of gadgets and pens just because they were free. And how many plastic grocery bags does one household really need? Also think of how many times you have bought something just to get the free item that it comes with. Think of the money you could save!

Do you have CDs and cassette tapes stacked around the house but you only like a few songs? Record your favorite songs on a single tape or CD. Short on time? Hire a high school student to record them for you.

If you spend 10 minutes a day looking for something, that equals about three days of your life a year. So if you live to be 80, that's 240 days of your life that you will have spent looking for things!

4

#3

Everything must have a home that's both easy to remember and to access.

Ask yourself, "What can I always find?" The answer is going to be something that is always put back after it is used. That's because it has a home that is both easy to remember and to access. For example: When I asked one client what she could always find, her immediate answer was her scissors. She kept them handle up in a mug with pens on the kitchen counter by the phone. Everyone in the house knew where to find them and they were all in the habit of putting the scissors back there when they were finished with them.

Next, ask yourself, "What can I never find?" This answer is going to be something that has not been given a home, or if it has a home that place is difficult to access. My client's example was her eyeglasses. Our next step was creating a system for it. One thing my client did was to purchase an eyeglass holder pin. This is a decorative pin that has a loop for one stem of the eyeglasses to slip onto. She puts the pin on in the morning and every time she takes off her glasses, she slips them onto the pin. Now she always knows where her glasses are. It was that simple.

The trick is to put something away in a place you will remember. Also you don't want to have to move anything to get to it. Make this easy to do and get in the habit.

#4

When in doubt, throw it out.

This one always gets some groans. That's because all of us have had the experience of throwing something away and then needing it the very next day. So there's a revision to this old adage. That is "box, tape, date and then dump." The way this works is that you box up all the items you're considering tossing out. Tape the box closed and put a date on it. Pick a date when you would feel comfortable throwing out the box, and its entire contents. Six months is usually a marker. Then mark the date on your calendar. When the day rolls around, toss the box out -- without looking at what it contains. Without looking is the key to the success of this program. If you untape the box and look inside, you're going to remember all the stuff you put in there and find reasons why you need to keep at least some of it.

A variation on the same theme is "use it or loose it." Decide on a period of time that you will keep something before discarding it. A year works well for most things; a season is good for clothing. If you have not used the item in that amount of time, then out the door it goes. Keep in mind that just because you're getting rid of it, does not mean you have to throw the item away. You can sell it at a consignment shop or donate it to one of a variety of places (some will even pick stuff up to). Keeping a bag in the bottom of your closets makes it easy to donate clothing items. Simply toss articles of clothing you no longer want into the bag. When the bag is full take it to a donation site or call to have a charity come and pick it up, some charities will even supply the bags!

Be leery of the garage sale pitfall. Saying you're collecting items to have a garage sale can create more clutter. If you don't have the sale in a timely manner, you could end up worse off than you started. Many times the sale never happens; garage sales are not as easy as they sound. And even if you do you can still be left with many of the items after the sale is over.

Lastly, keep a large garbage can in every room of your house -- preferably one without a lid, for easy access. The easier the garbage can is to use, the better chance that the clutter items will be thrown away.

Be aware of the feelings of fear or panic that can creep up while uncluttering your home. It's easy to keep items for fear that you'll regret getting rid of them. Or you may feel a need to keep everything. It can seem calming to have all your stuff around you. However it's exactly the opposite. The more stuff you have, the more work it takes to care for it all. Try the box trick for overcoming separation anxiety. It's a stress-free way to unclutter your home and to start living a simpler, uncluttered life.

80% of clutter in most homes is a result of disorganization -- not a lack of space.

Use plastic containers, baskets and boxes to keep like things together. This works for everything from kids' toy blocks to hair barrettes.

#5

Have a "do it now" attitude.

This can apply to everything. Just *do it now*. Hang up your clothes as you take them off (instead of letting a few days' worth pile up.) Put the laundry away as soon as it's folded (instead of letting clean laundry sit in piles around the house.) Sort through the mail when you bring it into the house (instead of letting a few days' worth sit there.) Make the phone call you have been putting off; schedule that appointment you have been meaning to make. Just do it. If you push the task off to be done later you'll still have to find the time. Just do it now.

☀ To avoid clutter buildup, get in the habit of spending ten minutes a night to un-clutter.

Keep in mind that de-cluttering is different from cleaning. De-cluttering is the task of placing everything back in its designated home. Cleaning is actually using a spray and rags to clean. You can be a very clean person who is disorganized; clean and neat are not the same. While working on a project you'll probably have what you need pulled out and spread around. That's messy. It's the organized person who can clear the mess in a snap by putting everything back where it belongs.

One way to make de-cluttering a little more fun is to challenge yourself or family members to see how much clutter can be organized in fifteen minutes. Actually set a timer and then start organizing. A lot can be done in a short amount of time. Finally, one last sure-fire way to clear a room or closet of clutter is to paint it. You will be forced to clear it out, before the painting begins.

By implementing only a few of these de-cluttering keys, you'll find yourself surrounded by a lot less stuff. You'll have more time and energy to do the things you want to do instead of moving piles of clutter from space to space.

🎩 Avoid having more than one of any item. If you have two pairs of reading glasses and you misplace one you will use the back up. But, if you have only one pair you will be forced to find it and to create a home for them so you will stop misplacing them.

Please refer to the Retention Schedule located in the back of the book.

Chapter Highlights

- Keep "like things" together.
- One in, one out.
- Everything must have a home.
- When in doubt, throw it out; otherwise known as "use it or lose it."
- Have a "do it now" attitude.

Chapter Resources

- National Assocation of Professional Organizers
  www.napo.net - 512-206-0151 - An assocation that
  offers referrals of professional organizers in your area.
- Solutions Catalog - www.solutionscatalog.com
  Toll Free – 1-877-718-7901
  P.O. Box 6878
  Portland, OR 97228
  A catalog full of time-saving, clutter-clearing ideas
- Lillian Vernon Catalog - www.lillianvernon.com
  800-545-5426 - A catalog with great household
  organizing items.
- Current Catalog - http://currentcatalog.com
  Current USA Inc. - 1-877-665-4458
  1005 East Woodman Road
  Colorado Springs, CO 80920 - A catalog that offers the
  eyeglass pin holder and many more great ideas.
- Life U Love - 1-866-294-9900
  369 Evergreen Blvd.
  Scotch Plains, NJ 07076
  www.lifeulove.com – jamie@lifeulove.com

**Next you have to be able to see
your dining room table.
AKA Household Management**

This section is for you if:

> ➤ You're embarrassed when friends drop by because the house is messy.
> ➤ You cannot find your dining room table under the piles of paper.
> ➤ Your laundry pile stands higher than your youngest child.

Or if you answer "yes" to any of the following:

> ➤ My life is full of unnecessary clutter and complexities.
> ➤ My bills are rarely paid on time.
> ➤ I put things down and have trouble finding them again.
> ➤ My car's maintenance is overdue.
> ➤ My garage is so full that I have to park the car in the driveway.
> ➤ Clothes in my closet need to be ironed before I can wear them.

- ➢ I forget birthdays and other important events.
- ➢ I (or my family members) am (are) overdue for medical and/or dental exams.

Introduction

Let's start this chapter with a quick quiz.
How many of these items can you find in 60 seconds or less?

- ➢ The phone book
- ➢ A deck of cards
- ➢ A flashlight
- ➢ Your last bank statement

- ➢ Candles and matches
- ➢ Your car title
- ➢ A working pen
- ➢ Band-Aids

Also do you have a system for these?

- ➢ Writing phone messages
- ➢ Signing permission slips
- ➢ Giving out lunch money
- ➢ Paying bills

- ➢ Ensuring that everything your children need gets to school with them.
- ➢ Sorting mail

You'll be able to find all those things on the list and have systems for everything after reading this chapter.

Are you embarrassed to have people over? When you know they're coming, do you pile things up or toss them into bags that you hide in the closet? You are not alone! Here are some great household management ideas -- broken down by topic and listed alphabetically -- that will help you get it all together.

Attic

While this is probably a place you rarely go, it should be kept as neat as any other space in your house. All of the boxes should be labeled. Label every side of the box; that way no matter how the box is stored, you'll know what's inside. When you're storing away items in boxes, leave room to add more. If you stuff the box full, then it will be more tempting to leave an item lying around than to start a whole new box. Lastly, consider color-coding the boxes by using plastic tubs with a colored lid. That way you will quickly be able to tell the Christmas decorations from old baby clothes. Rubbermaid makes some great storage containers and they came in a wide variety of shapes, sizes and colors.

 Label boxes "Christmas, 1 of 3" and so on.

Automobile

Keep your car up-to-date on its maintenance; routine repairs cost less than emergencies. Make sure now that your car is not due for any maintenance or inspection. Does anything need replacing? Do all the bulbs work? Are the wiper blades in good working order?

Here is a basic car maintenance checklist:

- ❏ Tune the engine

- ❏ Test all lights to make sure they're working. Clean the lenses

- ❏ Check treads on tires

- ❏ Air Filter

- ❏ Examine the washers and make sure the washer fluid bottle is filled with anti-freezing fluid. Put a jug of extra washer

- ☐ Have exhaust system checked
- ☐ Check battery cables
- ☐ Rotate tires

Additionally, there are other items you should have stored in your car to use when you need them. Many of these items can be stored neatly either in the trunk or glove compartment using organizers specifically designed for those areas.

Glove compartment:

- ☐ tissues
- ☐ aspirin
- ☐ deodorant
- ☐ car registration and insurance card
- ☐ breath freshener
- ☐ pens and paper
- ☐ cologne
- ☐ a small flashlight
- ☐ straws
- ☐ wipes
- ☐ bank withdrawal/deposit slips
- ☐ tire pressure
- ☐ small snacks
- ☐ gauge
- ☐ car manual

Inside car:

- ☐ paper towels
- ☐ supply of fresh water (change often)
- ☐ small trash can (use Velcro to keep it from sliding)

Trunk:

- ☐ Inflate-a-tire spray
- ☐ Extra paper towels
- ☐ A paintbrush, to use after a trip to the beach (to easily brush sand off you feet.)
- ☐ Towels for the beach or gym
- ☐ Durable, large snacks

- ❏ Emergency kit (including items like jumper cables, a large flashlight, a large "help" sign, flares, a first-aid kit.)
- ❏ Comfortable change of clothes (old sneakers, socks, sweats, etc.) You can change from a nice suit to sweatpants to check under the hood. Or you could switch from high heels to sneakers so you can walk more easily for assistance.

Keep a box in the trunk or back seat, filled with toys and games that kids can use in the car.

Basement
Install shelves in the basement so you can store and retrieve items easily. Consider using a dehumidifier if your basement is damp to avoid damage to stored items. All of the boxes should be labeled. Label every side of the box, that way no matter how the box is stored; you'll know what's in it. Lastly, consider color-coding the boxes by using plastic tubs with a colored lid. With color-coding you'll quickly be able to tell the good china from the old baby clothes.

Bathroom
Keep at least one set of spare towels in the bathroom along with extra paper products. You can even keep cleaning supplies in the bathroom for easy reach when you want to do a quick touchup. Also make sure there's a large garbage can in the bathroom for easy use and dumping consider not using the lid.

A small basket or rack can be used to house reading material such as magazines. A great way to organize and store small items, like hair accessories, is to place them in small baskets or decorative containers. Baskets also work well for all your nail care items. That way, you only have to grab one basket instead of hunting down the polish, cotton balls and nail files. You can place organizers into every drawer and even install some on the inside of cabinet doors. There are organizers specially designed to hold blow dryers and curling irons -- cords and all.

Unless everyone in your family uses the same shampoo and conditioner, chances are your shower gets pretty crowded. Shower caddies are a great way to get rid of the clutter. Everyone in the family gets a plastic tub to place all their items in. They carry the caddy into the shower with them and then back out, no more bathroom shower clutter. When not in use, the caddies can easily be stored on a shelf in the linen closet.

 Store scrunchies on a cardboard toilet-paper roll.

Bedroom
Make a rule that the last one up makes the bed and keep a spare set of sheets in the bedroom. Trunks and baskets make great decorative storage areas. Also consider using a shoe organizer. They're made specifically for all those shoes that can never seem to stay organized any other way. Lastly, make sure there's a large garbage can in the bedroom. For easy use, consider not using the lid.

Closets
Take a look in your closets and seriously consider installing a complete closet organizer yourself or hiring a professional to do it for you. Once you have an organizer in place, everything in the closet will have a home. There will be no more avalanches when a closet door is opened or endless searching for an article of clothing.

Also keep in mind that the closet should be well lit; this makes it much easier to find and replace things. There are battery-operated lights you can stick up if you don't have a light fixture already in place. In addition you might tie a ribbon, twist a twist tie, or wrap a rubber band around a hanger to indicate the navy items.

It will be easier for you to find articles of clothing if you keep "like things" together. For example, keep all the skirts next to each other and all your casual pants separate from your dress pants.

Lastly, keep a bag in the bottom of the closet where you can toss items that you're going to be donating. Once the bag is full, you can call to have a charity near you pick it up. Or you might prefer to place it in the trunk of your car. Then you could drop off the next time you're near a donation site.

I once worked with a client who invested in all areas of her life and home. She took excellent care of herself, taking time for things like massages. Her home was how she liked it, beautiful landscaping and well organized, in almost every area. As we walked through her home, she showed me the many changes she had made to help things run smoother. She had installed shelves and baskets on the walls to hold items that were used often. She had a kitchen table built that housed a turntable in the center. Then we opened a closet in her bedroom. Clothing was piled, there were stacks of laundry to be put away and the top shelves were empty because she could not reach them. "What's going on here?" I asked. "Oh, well I hardly see this, I just grab my clothes in the morning." But the more we talked about it, the more she realized it was important. She was wasting valuable time ironing clothes because they wrinkled sitting in the piles. She came to understand that even the places we rarely see need care too. She hired a professional closet organizing company to come in and build her shelving units. The closet organizers were made specific to meet her needs. The organizers held everything in just the right way and there was no wasted space.

 Hang belts on nails hammered into the closet wall.

Computer

The files in the family computer can get just as disorganized and hard to find as anything else in the house. By giving each family member their own folder, you can start to clean up the files. Each person saves their necessary files inside their folder and then they can easily retrieve them.

And it seems as though most Internet sites require you to register with a user name and password. It can be a challenge trying to remember all this information. So as often as possible, choose the same user name and password. Then jot down the information in a Rolodex or address book designated for the Internet. Take QVC for example. You can put QVC.com under the Qs and note your user name and password. You may also want to jot down their 1-800 number in case you need to contact them. The next time you log on to browse or do some shopping you'll have all the necessary information at your fingertips. You won't waste time looking for scraps of paper or trying out variations of your name to guess what you chose.

Crafts

Crafts and other hobbies can create enormous amounts of clutter. This can range from loose scraps of material for upcoming projects to unfinished projects you left out. Here are some ways to keep a handle on your craft clutter.

Use color-coded labels or color-coded box lids to keep different types of items for different projects. You could get clear-view plastic boxes with different color lids; use the red for sewing, green for knitting, and so on. And with the clear view, you'll be able to quickly see what's inside.

Also utilize your wall space; put up shelving and label the shelves with the names of the different types of project materials you have. This makes it easier to put items away and you can easily tell what you are out of. Baskets also fit well on most shelving and they can keep items handy. In utilizing your wall space, there are organizers that you can purchase too; some are even made to house specialty craft items. For example: A thread rack will keep your thread organized and easy to use. In addition, you might tack up a corkboard at eye level to pin instructions or patterns.

If you have a lot of fabrics, you can put up a clothing rod and hang the fabric pieces from the rod. For shorter fabric lengths and other more bulky items like batting and yarn, you can slip plastic grocery bags over the rod and put the items in the bag. Purchase magazine holders from an office supply store to keep books, instructions and patterns organized.

Desk
You're running a household, so the first thing you need is a desk. Sorry, but you can no longer use the dining room table to stack papers and then push them aside when it's time to set the table for dinner. Be creative when choosing a desk. It doesn't have to be a traditional desk; you can buy an ornate one. Or if space is tight, consider a desk that folds up or can be rolled out of a room.

Your desk or "command center" needs to be stocked with the following items:

- ❏ Paper
- ❏ Sticky notes
- ❏ Ruler
- ❏ Scissors
- ❏ Crayons
- ❏ Glue or glue stick
- ❏ #2 pencils
- ❏ Colored pencils
- ❏ Pencil sharper
- ❏ Stapler
- ❏ Extra staples
- ❏ Staple remover
- ❏ Tape
- ❏ Calculator
- ❏ Other items you use daily

Keep extras of any items in a storage location. Do not overstock the desk; this would cause clutter. Extras are easy to keep in a plastic bin that you slide under the desk. That way, replacements are always easy to access.

Trays can help to keep papers organized while they're out for a good reason. For example, you may have a shallow tray for papers to be signed. Your children could place anything that needs your signature in that tray and you can return it to them by the due date.

Schedule time in your day to sit down and address paperwork. By adding a few minutes every day to your routine, you can avoid large pileups of paperwork. It's much better to take five minutes to deal with and then file papers every day. You don't want to watch a pile of papers grow day after day knowing you'll eventually have to deal with it. You'll avoid the guilt when you get to it daily.

Disaster Preparedness
One way to reduce your stress is to be prepared for emergencies. Here are some simple steps you can take to be ready in the event of a disaster. Have a flashlight on hand with new batteries; you can store the batteries upside down in the flashlight to prevent it from turning on in storage and draining the batteries. Keep two gallons of bottled water on hand. Make sure that important and irreplaceable documents are stored in a fireproof box.

Some documents you might want to store are:

- Automobile insurance card(s) and policy(s)
- Birth certificate(s)
- Car registration(s) and title(s)
- Bank account numbers
- Deeds
- Copy of driver's license
- Homeowner's policy
- Irreplaceable photos
- Life insurance policy
- Investment records
- Mailing list of family and friends
- Marriage certificate
- Insurance cards and polices
- Medical history
- Military records
- Pin numbers
- Residency letter (a letter sent to you at current address to prove you reside there)
- Social security cards
- Tax records
- Will/living will

Another safety measure is to designate a family meeting place in the event family members cannot get home. You can choose a local house of worship or even a store or school. Also practice fire drills so children know what to do in case of a fire. Have all the family members gather in the driveway or somewhere else that's a safe distance from the house.

Lastly, if you have small children, you may want to institute a nickname policy. You would give each child a nickname or password of sorts. Then say for some reason you're unable to pick them up after school and you send someone else. That person will use the password or their nicknames so the children will know it's safe to go with that person.

Drawers

Use organizers to create separate spaces in drawers for different items. This will also prevent items from moving around as you open the drawer. Place the most used items in the front of the drawers and the least used items in the back. This is opposed to placing the most used items in the top drawer. It's more difficult to reach the back of a drawer and harder to see what's in there.

Environment

Because we're in our environment every day, we can become desensitized to it. Take a good look around you. Is your home the way you want it? Is it decorated the way you want it? Is it clean and neat and kept the way you want it? Are you living where you want to be living (in the area of the world, in the neighborhood you want)? Is your home exactly what you want it to be?

Errands

Make use of any pickup and delivery services. Many companies now offer this -- most at no charge. For example, pharmacies will often drop off prescriptions. Instead of you running out to drop shirts to the drycleaners, inquire about any pickup and delivery service they may offer. And instead of you lugging around a case of printer paper, why not just have the office supply store drop it at your doorstep? Sometimes even if there is a nominal charge for the service, it can be worth the small fee. Also, weigh the cost against the aggravation of getting everyone in the car and running over there yourself.

In addition, surf the Internet; many items can be easily and safely ordered online. Books, flowers, pet care items, drugstore items, groceries and gifts -- just to name a few!

Lastly, if you are going to run the errands yourself and you have small kids, consider paying a babysitter to come over for an hour. That way you can run all your errands at one time without the kids tagging along.

Create an "out basket" to place by the front door for errands. In this box you could put dry cleaning to be dropped off, library books to be returned, letters to mail, things to copy, and so on.

Consider hiring a college student to do routine tasks like grocery shopping, yard work and other household chores. This can free up as much as 20 hours a week!

Get stamps from an ATM machine or have them delivered. To order stamps just call the U.S. Postal Service at 800-782-6724.

Family Meetings

These meetings are a great way to discuss plans with everyone in the same place at the same time. I know a few families that start out family night with a meeting. Afterwards they play games, watch a movie, or scrapbook by adding new photographs to albums.

Having an agenda planned ahead of time helps; it lets family members know what to expect. Also it allows them to add their own items to the list of topics to be talked about. You can write the agenda on your wipe board so it's easy for everyone to see.

Another good document for you to create and review at family meetings is a list of house rules that includes the consequences for not following them. Every family member should be given a chance to contribute to the house rules.

One family I worked with complained that the children had gotten in the habit of telling their parents about sports games, concerts, and other important events at the very last minute. Sometimes the night of the event or after the event had already started! One example they shared was one Saturday; their ten-year old son rushed into the kitchen and breathlessly announced that his soccer game had started ten minutes ago. He needed to be there and he had promised to give another teammate a ride to the game. Incidences like this frustrated the parents who wanted to remain involved in their children's lives. I suggested a weekly family meeting. They decided to meet every Wednesday for a healthy, take-out dinner and a family meeting. Everyone was responsible to come to the table with all upcoming information and updates on anything else going on. It took a few weeks, but once the children got into the habit of sharing all the information, the parents had everything they needed to make decisions about who would attend what. The family meetings put an end to the lack of communication that had once plagued their household.

Family Notebook

Use a three-ring notebook with dividers. This notebook will be used to keep all the papers family members often needs. Some suggested sections are:

➢ Take-out menus ➢ Friends' and family members' phone numbers and addresses ➢ A yearly calendar ➢ A list of birthdays ➢ Emergency phone numbers ➢ Chore list ➢ List of baby-sitters ➢ Manuals and maintenance schedules for appliances and electronics	➢ Sports practice schedules ➢ Blank grocery lists ➢ Menu planners ➢ Weeks planned menu (to avoid those "what's for dinner?" questions) ➢ Packing lists for vacation ➢ Sleep-over packing lists ➢ List of movies to rent ➢ Car maintenance schedules and a list of dates the maintenance is performed

As you can see the possibilities are endless. This notebook can become like a "bible" for your family. Imagine all the necessary papers all in one place right at your fingertips!

Keeping track of your own schedule can be challenging enough. But when you have a family, add in their schedules and things can become chaotic. One of the first families I ever set up with a family notebook still uses it today, five years later. We used the notebook to solve their scheduling issues, missing paperwork problem and to control their clutter. This family came to me after having missed more than one soccer practice, showing up late for a family wedding and unable to find important paperwork without a long search. When I sat down with them they told me a story about a Saturday in their house a few weeks ago. The son needed his permission slip for a class trip to the museum Monday morning. He insisted that he had given it to his mother and she had misplaced it. Together they searched through piles of papers on the dining room table and towards the bottom of one pile the Mom came across an invitation, she undid the ribbon closure and read the invitation. It was then that she remembered that they were supposed to be at her cousin's wedding, an hour away, at 12. She checked the clock; it was 10:30! The family made a mad dash to get ready. They arrived at the wedding, a little late and very stressed. It was this incident that caused them to create a new system. Now when they receive invitations the information is put on the family calendar in the notebook. And the gift and card are purchased ahead of time. Each night at dinner the family reviews the next days events and confirms plans.

Garage
To start with, you can set up shelving around the perimeter of the garage. The shelving can hold items like all your car-care items or gardening tools. Car-care items fit nicely in a

24

bucket; you can toss in rags, cleaners, sponges and more. Label the shelves so everyone knows where things go back to when they're done with them.

And don't forget about all the hanging space that you have. You can hang bicycles, ladders, sports equipment and more with easy screw-in hooks. Another great way to hang things is from a pegboard. Tack up the board and you can easily hang tools.

To separate small items like nails and bolts, you can use a caddy with small pullout drawers or place them in jars that you can label with masking tape. And if you have sporting equipment, beach-going items and or lawn decorations, store them in sturdy plastic tubs with lids. Label the tubs or use a color-coding system like red lids for holiday items.

Lastly, place a mat by the door leading into the house for holding muddy shoes. This helps keep dirt from being tracked inside.

Garage Sales
The following are great ideas if you actually follow through and have a garage sale. Otherwise you're simply storing junk.

> Plan one with the neighbors; the larger the sale, the more people you will attract.
> Choose a weekend when weather is usually at its best and people should be around (holiday-weekend garage sales usually bomb).
> Put up and then take down easy-to-read signs that are protected in case it rains.
> If you don't want early birds showing up for the best deals, then state "No early birds" on your sings.
> Consider setting items in a large box and labeling the box "any item for $1.00" or set up a table the same way.

- To entice buyers to stay around a little longer, offer or sell doughnuts and coffee.
- Run a towel with Amoral or another polishing cream over plastic items to make them shine.
- Lastly, and most importantly schedule, a charity to come pickup the leftovers to prevent the items from reentering your home!

At a garage sale you need to have some change on hand to start with. A good amount is two $10.00 bills, six $5.00 bills, twenty $1.00 bills and $10 in assorted change. Placing the coins in a muffin tin makes it easy to see where the coins are.

Garden

First, designate one place where you'll be keeping all your gardening paraphernalia -- the garage, a shed, or the basement. Then separate the tools into four sections (work, water, weed, and reap.) Use easy-to-get-into baskets, bins, buckets or tubs to keep each type of tool. Labeling the bins makes it easy to put tools back where they belong. A pegboard is another good way to keep gardening items. You can hang your tools and that makes them easy to see and access.

Smaller items like gloves, a hat, trowel and clippers are easy to carry back and forth to the yard when stored in a basket with a handle. A rubber bucket, garden tote bag or a garden tool belt can be used to carry tools to and from the garden.

There's another great gardening product on the market. It's a rolling bench. The seat lifts up and you can store tools inside. That way, all your tools are with you when you need them. The bench is easy to move around and you can sit instead of kneeling while gardening.

Gifts/Cards

Keep a file (or a list in your organizer) of good ideas for gifts for yourself or others. Add to this as you come across new items. When you need to buy a gift or give someone suggestions for yourself, refer to the file or list. For example when you're asked what you would like as a gift, you might suggest disposable gifts with meaning like homemade cookies, tickets to a show, or a gift certificate good for a service like a manicure.

Keep a few generic gifts on hand and ready to give; candles and gift certificates that do not expire are always good. Keep gift bags in stock too. And easily store rolls of wrapping paper without ripping or crinkling them by using a gift-wrap storage container; there are some great ones that slide right under the bed. Then when you need to get a gift ready in a rush, you won't have to stop at a store. You can just go to your gift-related stash.

Along the same lines, keep a card caddy with cards for all occasions including some blank ones. Go to the store and pickup cards for all occasions, birthdays, anniversaries, weddings, baptisms and more. The next time you need to mail out a card, you'll have some at your fingertips. And to remember to send out the cards in time, either place a note on your calendar or place the cards in your tickler file.

Grocery Shopping/Meal Planning

Before you go grocery shopping, plan out your meals for the next one to two weeks. Plan what you'll be fixing and compare that to what you have in the house so you know what you need to buy. Decide ahead of time which brands you'll buy; this prevents you having to stand in front of rows of toothpaste trying to pick one. Keep the meal plans and shopping lists to reuse them in the future. Once you know what you're cooking for the week, write the meals on the family calendar; your family will then know what's for dinner?

When you're cooking a meal that will reheat well, like lasagna, make double and freeze the extra. That way, on a night when time is tight, you can heat that up instead of driving by the fast food window. Slow cookers or Crock-Pots make good meals and take little time. Once you toss the ingredients in during the morning, you can let it cook all day and a homemade meal is waiting for you at the end of the day. Rice cookers are a great way to make the starch for the meal, it's quick and easy.

Please refer to the Grocery Meal Planning and Master Grocery Shopping List located in the back of the book.

I once worked with a client family where both parents worked and there were three teenage children in the house. But the mother was the one who rushed home from work to prepare the dinner meal for the whole family. If you live in a house that sounds something like this, you might consider doing what this family did. My client family held a family meeting and the mother explained that she was feeling a lot of pressure to get home from work to prepare a meal that everyone would enjoy. She asked for some suggestions on ways the whole family could help out. Here is what they came up with. Mom and Dad would grocery shop together every Tuesday evening. No more stops every day on the way home from work to pick up that night's dinner. Everyone agreed to be responsible for adding items they needed to a master grocery list. And if the item was not on the list they would have to wait to get it until the next shopping trip the following Tuesday. Mom would cook the meals on Mondays and Saturdays. Each of the children agreed to be responsible for one dinner one night a week on Tuesdays, Wednesdays, and Thursdays. The family would buy take-out or go out to eat on Fridays. And Dad would pitch in by cooking a meal on Sundays and when he made his meal on Sunday if it was something that would freeze and reheat well, he would make double. Mom bought a crock-pot and a crock-pot recipe book so everyone had the option to make a crock-pot meal. By simply tossing in all the ingredients in the morning and leaving it on low all day, there was a healthy, tasty meal ready at dinnertime. It took a few weeks before the system ran smoothly, but once they got it down pat it worked really well. Not only was the pressure off Mom, but the children were learning to cook, gaining more responsibility and Dad became more involved with managing the household.

Coupons: unless you're really going to use them, they are a waste of time, create clutter, and trigger guilt. Be honest with yourself, or it can cause you a lot less unnecessary stress.

Cook interactive meals. Example: homemade individual pizzas. Everyone can pick his or her own toppings. Other possibilities include tacos or a baked potato bar.

Make a list of the most used grocery items in your house, and then make fifty-two copies. Place one on the refrigerator weekly. Then all you have to do is to circle what you need instead of writing it out. Prepare a list before you go shopping to avoid the dreaded "oh no, I forgot..." and try to buy only what's on your list. If it's not on the list the day you shop, then it waits until the next week. Carry your coupons with you; the organizers made just for that work great. Shop during off-peak hours; lines are shorter and shelves are more stocked. Try not to grocery shop when you're hungry. You end up buying stuff not on your list. Lastly, consider shopping with a friend and buying in bulk so you can share the groceries and the cost.

Cook extra at dinner. Broiling chicken breasts? Make extra and prepare chicken breast sandwiches or chicken salad for lunch the next day.

Before you toss out an empty food container, add the item to your shopping list.

Holidays/Parties
Cooking, parties, shopping, cleaning, decorating, and wrapping -- the list goes on and on. But remember, you're not in competition with anyone. Make the holidays yours, start some new traditions and create gatherings that are less stressful. Arrange events so that you can spend the maximum amount of time with company and not slaving over a hot stove. For example, you can have everyone bring a dish and then you only have to make a few items. This allows people to feel useful and frees up time for you. Another new tradition might be to buy some Christmas cookies and only make the really unusual ones or the ones everyone loves.

Whatever you decide to do, remember the holidays are not about the parties, food and gifts. They're about the people in your life and being thankful that you know them.

Consider keeping a holiday journal where you can jot down what the holidays were like, who gave and received what gifts, and what the menu was. That way, the next year, you can avoid giving the same gifts and you can review the menu to see what was popular.

To avoid writing out all your holiday cards, print labels for them off your computer.

When the holidays are over, take a moment to review. Jot down what you regret not making the time to do. Then clip the paper to next years calendar so next holidays season you can make the time.

Too many people to shop for? Consider making agreements not to buy for everyone. Instead place the names of everyone exchanging gifts into a hat and everyone pick one. That way you don't have to buy a ton of gifts, but everyone gets something. Avoid agreeing to "only buy for the children." The children will get plenty of gifts and besides, adults like getting gifts too.

Lots of shopping can be done over the Internet or through a catalog. If the gift is for someone out of state, consider having the gift shipped directly to him or her. Refer to your gift file, where you have tossed all those great gift ideas as you saw them throughout the year.

Shop Monday thru Friday from 8 AM to 5 PM when most people are at work. Try not to shop at lunchtime, in the evening or on the weekends, when everyone else is out there. Take one personal day off from work to shop all day. Leave the kids at home; even if you have to hire a babysitter, shopping without kids is much less stressful. If you're shopping with a friend, consider having their kids come over to your house. Then a babysitter can watch all the children at one house and you can split the cost.

Wrap the gifts as soon as you buy them and put the to/from labels on immediately. This prevents having stacks of gifts to wrap at the last moment. Use pack-and-send services to avoid those long post office lines at the holiday.

Designate one place in your house to be Gift-Wrap Central. At this spot, keep scissors, tape, wrapping paper, boxes, gift bags, to/from tags, tissue paper, and bows and ribbons.

Book your babysitter as soon as you know about an upcoming event; good babysitters book up early.

Writing out holiday cards can be another daunting task that ends up feeling more like a chore then a warm holiday pastime. Here are some ideas to help make the task a little more enjoyable.

> First, type your holiday card list into the computer; then you can mail merge and print labels instead of handwriting all those envelopes.
> Consider typing up a family newsletter or a letter to family and friends to enclose in a card or send with one. You can update people on what has been happening with your family, wish them well in the New Year and tell them how glad you are that you know them. With current technology, it's simple to add a family photo to the letter.
> You could send a holiday postcard instead of an actual card. This saves you on time and postage. A clever and unusual postcard is to take a family photo and print them in 4x6 size. Then address them on the right-hand side and write a note on the left-hand side. Add on postage and you're set.

Whatever you decide to send out, don't sit down to write them all out at once. Break up the task and only write a few a night. For example, maybe do one letter of the alphabet each night.

For unique and easy "thank you" notes, take a picture of everyone attending a party, then get 4x6 copies made. Write your "thank you" note on the back on the left-hand side, address the right-hand part. Pop on postage and you're set.

Home Office

Working out of your home on a daily basis or occasionally can be a blessing, however it can also blur the lines between your work and home life. Here are some ways to keep your home office from taking over your life.

Post your work hours and stick to them. Dress for work and change when you're done working for the day. Use two different colored phones -- one for work and one for home -- so you don't accidentally answer the office line with a simple "hello."

Another challenge that plagues home offices is a lack of space. Use the space you do have wisely. Utilize wall space; consider shelves to keep supplies and organizers to keep the shelves neat. And purchase office machines which serve more than one purpose – Example: a fax that can also copy, print and scan.

Housecleaning

The less stuff you have, the less time it will take you to clean it all. Also, to keep cleaning to a minimum, avoid buying items that require extra work -- like silver that needs polishing.

Create a cleaning caddy using a plastic tub or a container with a handle. Place your cleaning supplies in there -- gloves, rags, cleaners and more. Then you can just tote the caddy along with you as you go from room to room. To avoid having a caddy filled with all different types of cleaners, try to choose multi-purpose cleaners, they save you money too.

Keep a spot cleaner for your rugs handy. When something spills, dab on the cleaner right away. This avoids having to scrub the entire rug. Also, invest in a powerful hand vac; it's much simpler to use when there is a small spill.

You can avoid having to clean some areas if you clean as you go. For example: If you rinse the sink after brushing your teeth, there will be no leftover toothpaste that needs to be scraped off. This saves you both time and energy because almost everything is easier to clean right away.

Remember, you're not the only one who is capable of dusting, vacuuming, filling or emptying the dishwasher, and doing other housework chores. Divide up the chores between family members and jot them on the calendar. Everyone in the family participates in making the messes; it's only fair that they be involved in the cleanup as well. Make a detailed list of exactly what needs to be done. Instead of asking someone to clean the bathroom, ask him or her to scrub the tub, wipe the mirrors, swish the toilet, wipe the counters, wash the floor, clean the sink and put out fresh towels.

Please refer to the Stain Buster Sheet located in the back of the book.

To get your younger children excited about helping out around the house, consider hiding change or small toys. Choose a place where they will need to dust or sweep to do a thorough cleaning job. Or use a timer to make a game of cleaning up.

"Your children won't remember how clean their childhood home was, but they will always have memories of how much time you spent playing with them." Author Unknown

To clean stains from the bottom of a vase, fill it with water and drop in two Alka-Seltzer tablets.

If you make it a habit not to wear shoes in the house, there will be a lot less cleaning to do. Consider placing a large box for shoes by the front door and keeping slippers and socks there.

When you're doing a thorough cleaning, tackle the job in an organized way. Have everything you need handy. Start in one corner of the room and work your way around. When you come across something that belongs in another room, don't take it there right away. Just make a pile or basket of stuff that belongs somewhere else. Then take it there when you're done. If you keep going back and forth between rooms, you'll waste time. You'll also run the risk of getting involved in another project.

Keep extra garbage bags in the bottom of the can. When you empty one, the new one will be handy.

"Zone cleaning" works well. For instance, you can give the bedrooms a thorough cleaning one weekend, leaving the dining room and kitchen until the next weekend. Remember that the house does not need a thorough cleaning each and every week. It's perfectly acceptable to do a speed cleaning when you just want to touch up. And for the real heavy duty cleaning, like a spring-cleaning, consider hiring someone to help you. Cleaning companies have the employees, products and energy to tackle the tough once-a-year jobs.

Spring-Cleaning "To Do" List

- Wash windows
- Patch screens
- Check and clean out gutters
- Pain
- Spruce up siding
- Do needed caulking
- Touch-up the landscaping
- Clean/oil door locks
- Sweep chimney
- Wash walls
- Oil woodwork
- Wax hardwood floors
- Clean the rugs
- Prepare grill for warm weather cook-outs
- Clean and fix patio furniture
- Clear deck of unneeded items and paint on a clear sealer coat if needed
- Clean and fix furniture
- Air out your house
- Check the play equipment
- Prepare the pool
- Freshen up the sandbox
- Change the air conditioner filter and make sure the air conditioner works
- Change the water filter on the main water line
- Flush household drains
- Refresh the power-outage emergency kit, including candles, matches, flashlight and fresh batteries

Note: If you live in warm weather year-round, some items on the spring and summer lists may not apply to you.

Winterize House "To Do" List

- Get heating system tuned up
- Pull refrigerator from the wall and clean condenser coils in the back with a vacuum cleaner using the brush attachment

- Refresh the power outage emergency kit, including candles, matches, flashlight and fresh batteries
- Seal the driveway
- Check for gaps in rubber-stripping around doors

The Department of Energy estimates that the average homeowner wastes $350 a year on heating bills because of inefficient insulation.

Remember, in the overall scheme of things, a clean house isn't really all that important.

A client had a plaque hanging on her wall that read, "Cleaning and scrubbing can wait till tomorrow for babies grow up we've learned to our sorrow. So quiet down cobwebs and dust go to sleep. I'm rocking my baby and babies don't keep."

Kids' Rooms/Toys
You can keep the mess in the children's rooms under control by having everyone agree to the following two rules:

1. One thing out at a time.
2. One new toy in, one old toy out.

Bookshelves make great holding areas for all sorts of stuff, not just books. Make sure older kids have a desk that is stocked with supplies just like yours. Also, have a two-drawer filing cabinet so older children can file away old reports, projects, homework and artwork. Prepare homework caddies that include all the items each child commonly needs to complete his or her homework.

Use the higher shelves in the closet to store things while leaving the lower shelves available for things a child uses most. Have a laundry bin in each child's room next to the closet. If the child is old enough, have him or her sort the laundry and get the bin to the laundry room the night before laundry day.

A great way to store childhood mementoes is to place a chest at the foot of the child's bed; you can keep artwork, report cards and other keepsakes in there. That way, they can take the whole chest with them when they go out on their own. Take a photograph of large projects, like dioramas, that cannot easily be stored.

Lastly, make sure there is a garbage can in each child's room that is easy to reach and large enough to handle his or her trash.

Clear plastic shoeboxes work great for storing toys. Place them on bookshelves or store them easily under the bed.

Ever hear a child complain, "There's nothing to do"? Solve this complaint by helping the child write and post a "nothing to do" list. It can include things like, make Grandma a picture or read a book. Next time your hear that tired phrase, direct the child to the list.

In a child's room, one client created a time line. This included the child's birth date, when the first tooth arrived, date of the first walk, etc. Now the child can go back and see what happened. This client and her child can record new milestones and tell stories as they look at the time line.

Help your kids create checklists of things to do before leaving for school. Include things like "check for homework in backpack" and "brush teeth." Consider posting the checklists on their bedroom walls or by your front door:

Checklist for School

_____	Make sure I have all my homework
_____	Get lunch box/lunch money
_____	Locate textbooks
_____	Find any library books to return
_____	Get permission slips
_____	Where am I going after school? What will I need?
_____	Do my parents know where I am going?
_____	Give my parents all notes/messages from teachers
_____	Do I have gym today? Do I need clothes?
_____	Do I need my team uniform for practice?
_____	Do I have my musical instrument for my lesson?

Kitchen/Pantry

You can organize your kitchen in a very logical fashion. You can have the cabinet with the dishes be the cabinet closest to the dishwasher. That way as you pull out clean dishes, you're right near where they go to be put away. The same goes for cabinets with pots and pans; those can be closest to the stove for cooking. And think of the best way to store the items. Pans work well stored vertically and lids are easy to find if they are in a lid organizer. Organize your kitchen in a way that works for you.

Organize your spices according to how often you use them. For example: Salt, pepper, garlic powder and paprika may be right out in front. Other spices, like cumin could be far in the back. In contrast with the alphabetical system, cumin would be right up front.

Clean as you cook. If you are making lasagna, while waiting for the pasta water to boil you could be sauce the pan and then rinse the spoon. And if you drip sauce, wipe it up immediately. By keeping up with the dishes and spills as the meal cooks, you can avoid having a sink full of dirty dishes and a messy counter top before the meal is even served.

Take a look at what you have out in your kitchen. Are there appliances that you hardly use taking up valuable counterspace? If so, put them in cabinets or on a shelf in your pantry. You can store your canisters in cabinets also to save counterspace. Designate each drawer to hold something. One drawer can be for all the cooking instruments and so on.

Use organizers whenever possible. There are organizers for clear plastic wrap and aluminum foil. There are others for over the sink and many designed for use inside the refrigerator. There are some great refrigerator ones that use wasted space to hold cans of cold soda. Another trick is to get a plastic box and put all the items you use to make a sandwich in there. Store this in the refrigerator. Then instead of pulling out the mayonnaise and lunchmeats and pickles, you can reach for the single sandwich caddy.

Label the shelves in the pantry. Group similar items together on the shelves – such as soups, canned vegetables, condiments and baking supplies.

Place a lazy susan in the center of your kitchen table during dinner; it avoids everyone having to pass items around, especially helpful if the bowls are hot.

Tape an equivalent measures chart and substitutions chart on the inside of a cabinet. Post a favorite recipe or two there as well.

Use your drawer space wisely. Put the most commonly used items in the front of the top drawer. Then place the second most used items in the front of the second drawer, not in the back of the top drawer. It's easier to get to the front of the second drawer than to reach to the back of the top drawer.

Toss out extra gadgets and gizmos. Do you have more than one egg separator or garlic press? Do you even use them? If not, toss them out or donate them.

Have a pair of kitchen scissors available. It makes cutting foods like lettuce and scallions a cinch.

Laundry/Wardrobe
It's important to keep the laundry room organized, whether the machines share part of another room or they have a room all to themselves. Shelving units help to keep the laundry room tidy. There are organizers specially made to fit between the washing machine and dryer, so no more clothes fall between the two machines.

Put a system in place for doing laundry; this helps to keep the task manageable. By designating one or two days a week as "laundry days," everyone gets in the habit of having their dirty clothes sorted and in the laundry room ready to wash on those days. If they do not have the clothes in the laundry room, then these clothes wait to be washed until the next laundry day. Also, have family members get in the habit of bringing their own laundry to the laundry room and sorting it. And they can also come to pickup their finished laundry and put it away themselves.

Read the care tags on clothes before you purchase them. Although linen may be appealing because it breathes, remember that it wrinkles easily. Watch for "dry clean only" items; they cost you more money and time in the long run. Choose "easy to wear and wash" fabrics that will last for seasons to come.

Give up fashion trends. Build a wardrobe around three colors. Have a few pairs of shoes that go with a lot.

Generally people wear only 20% of their outfits 80% of the time. Pear down you closets, save your favorite outfits, the ones that look and feel good. Donate the rest.

House Rules

If you take it out, put it back.
If you borrow it, return it.
If you open it, close it.
If you take it off, hang it up.
If you break it, fix it.
If you finish it, replace it.

Mail/Paper

The great paper chase – you're not alone; no one can seem to escape it. There are papers everywhere and they inexplicitly seem to multiply. So much for that paperless society so many people talked about. If anything, computers have created more paper. So how do you deal with it all? How do you keep from being buried underneath stacks or, more importantly, keep your kids permission slips and your bills from being lost with no hope of recovery?

Simple. Create a system for every paper that comes into your home. And it's not as difficult as you may think. First, let's stop some of the paper from ever entering your home by getting off junk mail lists for good. You can do this at no cost by mailing a letter to The Direct Marketing Association, Mail Preference Service, P.O. Box 9008, Farmingdale, NY 11735-9008. Be sure to include your name (and any variation of your name that you use), your address and a request to be removed from all mailing lists. Sign the letter and send it off. It will take a few weeks but you can see up to a 70% reduction in the amount of junk mail that you receive. Next, make a toll-free call requesting that you no longer receive the preapproved credit card offers. Dial 888-567-8688 and choose the permanent removal option, "#3." If you change your mind, you can always call back to have your name returned to the lists at a later date.

 Use a letter opener to open mail, it's quicker.

Change your check register on Dec. 31st so you can file it with that year.

On average, the disorganized person has 3000+ documents at home.

In 1952, Americans received the same amount of mail in one year as we now receive in one month.

If we all stopped receiving unwanted junk mail, we could save close to 100 million trees every year.

You cannot stop all mail from coming. So the key is to design a system for the necessary mail that you do receive. Go through your mail one time a day. Ideally you want to be sitting at your desk. That way, you'll have your organizer handy, the tickler file at your fingertips, and your "to read file" ready to be filled. You'll also be near the family notebook and bill-paying caddy. Plus you're sitting near the garbage can -- preferably with no lid for easy access -- and a shredder (shred any mail that includes your personal information on it.)

The average American gets 49,060 pieces of mail in a lifetime – one-third of it is junk.

Before we continue with the mail, let me introduce you to a few terms I just used that you might not be familiar with.

Tickler file
This is a forty-three-slot file that is looked at each and every day. It can be an accordion file, rolling file, one drawer designated only for the tickler file, or forty-three files in a carrying case. To create a tickler file, you take thirty-one files and label them 1 through 31, then take twelve files and label one for each month -- January through December.

Here's an example of how a tickler file works. Say that on April 1st you receive an invitation to a birthday party on April 8th and you plan on attending. First, you reserve the time and date by scheduling the time in your organizer. Then you write RSVP and the phone number on your "to do" list. Next, you place the invitation in the Saturday slot before the party, which in this case is April 6th. Then you can forget about the party and having to buy a gift because the tickler file will remind you. When April 6th comes, you'll open the file labeled 6 and find the invitation. You now are reminded that you need a gift and card. That weekend, you buy the gift and card (if you don't have any on hand). Place the invitation back in the tickler file but now in the file labeled 8. And on the 8th when you check the folder, you'll have the invitation in hand that has the phone number and directions to where you are going. Had the invitation been for a month later, May 8th, then you would have filed it in the May file. On May 1st, you would have reviewed the entire May file and filed items where they needed to be.

It really is that simple. It takes a little time to get into the habit. However, once you start using it, the tickler file is a no fail plan for remembering everything you need to remember.

To Read File
This is a file or an envelope that holds all those items that you have been hoping to get the time to read. The file can be a simple manila folder, a fancy plastic one with a rubber strap to hold it shut, or any other type of file that works for you. The "to read" file is where you place all those papers you want to get a chance to read that would usually end up in an unread stack somewhere at home. The "to read" file is what you carry with you when there's a good chance you'll have to wait for at least a few minutes. This might be waiting for you name to be called at the doctors' office, waiting to pick your child up from sports practice, or

waiting for a meeting to begin. Some people find it helpful to store a highlighter in their file in order to note the name under which the paper will be filed or to mark areas that need to be re-read.

Keep your "to read file" in a bag. Toss anything else in the bag that you might be able to take care of while you're waiting. Keep your "waiting bag" waiting by the front door on a small table, on a hook, or in some other handy place.

Bill Paying Caddy

This is a large basket or plastic caddy of some sort which houses all the items used when you're paying your bills. The usual items include:

- ➤ Stamps
- ➤ Return address labels
- ➤ A calculator

- ➤ Your checkbook
- ➤ A pen
- ➤ A pencil.

Now back to the mail. Let's look at sorting it.

Place all catalogs and sales flyers in a basket and empty the basket at the end of the month -- read or not. Or consider immediately tossing all the catalogs. Flipping through a catalog not only wastes your time, but it shows you things that you never knew you needed. Tossing them could save you money. If you need something, you can always find a place to buy it and, believe me, they will always be happy to send you another catalog. My advice is to toss all the catalogs you have lying around, plus all the new ones that come into your life.

When a magazine arrives in the mail, first stop and ask yourself if you have the time and desire to read it. If not, cancel the subscription immediately; you can always re-subscribe at a later date. However, if you do enjoy the articles, then scan the table of contents and rip out any of the articles that catch your interest. You're not going to read them now. Just staple them together and place them in your "to read" file for when you will have time to take a closer look.

Next, pull out all the bills, open them now, and only keep the bill and return envelope. Toss all the inserts and other useless paper they enclose. Place the bills in your bill paying caddy and move on to the rest of the mail.

Now, with each piece of mail you open, make a decision right then about it. Is it for someone else in the family? Then toss it in their bin, basket, tray or whatever you have designated as their in-box.

Ideally, you should only be touching a piece of paper once. I know it sounds unrealistic, but with a little practice, this can be accomplished with many items. Simply make a decision about the paper right then and there while it's in your hand. A good measuring tool to decide whether or not you should keep the paper is to ask yourself the following questions.

> Do I really need this?
> Do I have the information in some other format?
> Can I get the information again if I need to?

Papers usually fall into one of the following five categories:

> **To do today**: Put it on your "to do" list and place the paper in your organizer.
> **To do**: Place it in your tickler file; make any notes you need in your organizer.

- ➤ **Trash/recycle**: This one is the easy one; use it a lot!
- ➤ **To file**: Place in your bin or tray where you place items to be filed.
- ➤ **To pass on**: Put it into an envelope and address this so you can give/send the item to the right person.

 About 80% of what is filed is never looked at again.

Lastly, let's touch on filing. Be very selective about what you decide to file. When you need information, you can get it then and it will be current. Anyway, you probably will not remember that you filed the information. The less filed, the less stored. The less stored, the less to care for.

However, there are always papers that need to be kept. Some need to be kept in a fireproof box -- like birth certificates and a paid mortgage letter. Others simply get filed in some sort of order; we'll talk about that in a moment. A two, or four-drawer filing cabinet works well but there are other ways of keeping files. There are decorative boxes, wicker filing cabinets or rolling files that can simply be rolled under a desk when not in use. The key is to pick one way of filing and stick with it. There is no one right way, and no way is particularly better than another. There is only the way that works for you.

Filing Systems
There are basically two ways of setting up your filing system. First, there's the traditional way, where all the files are *alphabetized* in the drawers. For instance, you might choose to file by company name, working your way from A through Z. Or you can file by *topic*, which is the way that seems to work best for most households. An example of how filing by topic would work is this. You would take a hanging folder and label the tab "Insurance" (notice that I did not write it in all capitals; we read quicker when the word uses both upper and lower case). Then fill the

hanging folder with manila folders labeled for each type of insurance you have -- life, house, health, car and so on.

A great way to ensure that the files always stay in place and are filed correctly is to write on the outside of the manila folder which hanging folder it belongs in. Make it a rule never to remove the hanging folder. Then if you pull the car insurance folder, you can easily know where to re-file it. Another time saver is to color-code files. Use one color for each topic you have. Maybe all the financial files are green and the kids' schoolwork and projects are blue. Filing can be that simple.

Pets
All pets require care. All of the care can be shared by family members, and some can even be done by young children. Divide up the tasks and write who is to do what on what days on the family calendar. To make the chores a little easier, it's helpful to place everything a person needs in a single caddy or a plastic tub with handle. For example, a pet-feeding caddy would have food, treats, vitamins, towels for spills and anything else you might need to change the food. On the other hand, a cleaning caddy for a dog might contain shampoo, conditioner, towels, nail clippers, a brush and anything else needed for cleaning a dog. A cleaning caddy for a hamster might have the bedding chips, new wooden toys and anything else needed to freshen a hamster's cage.

Remember that routine visits to a veterinarian cost less then an unchecked problem that becomes an expensive emergency.

Lastly, just like kids, pets often have toys; the trick to keeping them from being scattered throughout the house is to toss them in a toy box. This can be a simple plastic crate or cardboard box.

Phone

Have you ever gotten the message that "so-and-so called a day ago"? I think we all have at some point. To avoid this you need to design a system for phone messages. The first part of the system should be to have pen and paper by every phone in the house. Then *everyone* needs to agree to be sure to write down phone messages. That is the key part. Then it's simply a matter of what to do with the messages. One option is to have a basket or tray for everyone and the message gets put there. Or you can have a board where all the messages get stuck. Whatever method you choose, there are two parts to its success. The message needs to get written down and everyone needs to know *where* to look to see if they have any messages.

"Oh, Mom? I forgot to tell you Mrs. Smith called the other night." Sound familiar? Without a system for phone messages it is no surprise when messages don't get relayed. This is what was happening with one of my client families. They consulted with me after a very important phone call got missed resulting in the father losing out on a big contract. So we instituted a system for each and every phone message. First we created a phone message sheet to be filled out when taking a message. The sheet had blank spaces for the date and time of the call. The name of the caller and the message. The paper was copied and a stack was placed in an organizer, with pens, beside each phone in the house. When a call came in for a person who was not home the procedure was for phone call sheet to be completely filled out. That way nothing would be forgotten. Then the sheet was immediately taken to the stack of in-boxes we placed on the family "command center" otherwise known as a desk. Everyone in the family agreed to either be responsible for each phone call they answered or they were not to answer the phone. For example, if they were in the middle of a project and would not be able to write the message down then the plan was to let the answering machine take the call. Remember just because the phone rings does not mean it has to be answered.

The next time you get your phone bill, take a close look at it. What extras do you have on the phone? Call waiting? A party line? Remote answering? Ask yourself if those features are used and if they are worthwhile. Back before all those fancy features were available, if someone called and got a busy signal, they'd just call back later. It was that simple. Now you have to put someone on hold if the call-waiting beeps, and then you are responsible for remembering to tell someone about the message or for returning the call yourself. This is complicated. We talked earlier about simplifying our lives. This is one way to do that, and it saves money in the process.

Lastly, pull out that annoying manual and take the time to program the speed dials buttons on your phone. It may not seem like a big deal but it's a huge time-saver. So take a few minutes and plug in the most commonly used numbers -- including emergency numbers.

Hang an organizer by the phone for keeping a few pens and paper handy.

Tell people that you only answer the phone from 7-8 PM. Use the answering machine at all other times. They will be more likely to call during that time, freeing up the rest of your evening.

Photographs

Pictures are a great way to capture those special moments. However they don't do you much good if they remain in undeveloped rolls of film scattered around your house or in envelopes of developed pictures in forgotten piles. Consider using a mail-away service to get the pictures developed and for reordering film. This saves you trips to the photo store and usually saves you money too. Then schedule time to go through your photos. Immediately toss any bad shots, double-exposures and pictures that make you wonder why you took them.

Find a storing system for the photographs that works for you. It may be labeling a shoebox and putting the pictures in there. You may want to put together a photo caddy; there you can keep the most recent scrapbook or photo album, along with tape or glue and markers for labeling the pictures. You might also keep a stash of blank envelopes here that way you can easily send some pictures to family members and friends so they can remember special moments too.

I know of a family who spends one night a month sitting around flipping through old pictures and placing new ones into albums. The whole family gets to relive memories and catch up on what has been happening in their lives while they organize the new photos. It does not feel like a chore.

When you organize your next batch of photos, do a few old ones at the same time. Just by starting you'll feel a lot better.

Recipes

The first step towards controlling recipe clutter is to look through all your recipes. Keep only the ones you intend to cook and try in the near future.

Here are some ideas on organizing all the recipes you have clipped out. Take a three-ring notebook and fill it with loose-leaf paper and dividers. Tape the recipes to the paper and file them under a category like main dishes, desserts, appetizers and so on. Another idea is an accordion file where you can categorize the recipes in the slots. A really easy way is to get a magnetic-pages photo album and put the recipes in the protective pages.

Try one recipe a week and keep only those that are a success.

Recycle
Depending on where you live, there are different rules for recycling items like paper, glass and plastic. You simply need a system for each of the items you recycle. Small tubs inside kitchen cabinets or decorative containers can house the recyclables inside the house. Later they can be brought outside and dumped into larger garbage cans.

Mark the family calendar with recycling dates. If you have curbside service, designate someone to be in charge of dumping the recycling outside into the large cans and getting it to the curb on recycling day. Otherwise, assign the task of taking the items to the recycling center.

A client was cleaning out her child's room and came across many teddy bears in good condition. Wondering what she might do with them all, she remembered she had heard of a "Teddy Bear Clinic" being held at the local hospital. She called and found out they were still accepting donations for the upcoming clinic. She donated the bears and after the clinic she received a thank you note telling her how successful the event had been. For those of you who may not be familiar with a "Teddy Bear Clinic." It is an event for children from the community when they can come to have the nurses and doctors from the hospital "fix" or repair their old, worn teddies. If the child does not have a teddy he or she is given one of his or her own. This helps children to be less fearful of medical professionals and hospitals. It also is a great way to give to the less fortunate, as many of the children without bears of their own do not have many toys at all.

Here are some places willing to help you recycle other items:

➢ **Bubble wrap, plastic foam, peanuts, and sturdy boxes: To Mail Boxes Etc.** or other pack-and-send locations.

➢ **Business clothes:** Bring women's suits, skirts, blouses and nearly new shoes to your local **Dress for Success**, an organization that outfits low-income women for job interviews. Visit www.dressforsuccess.org

➢ **Christmas cards:** Send to St Jude's Ranch for children makes new cards out of old and sells them to raise money.
PO Box 985
Boulder City, Nevada 89005

➢ **Computers:** If your old PC is a 486 or better, the **National Cristina Foundation** – 1-800-cristina; www.cristina.org will match the computer with a needy organization and pick it up from your home. To donate an ancient or nonworking computer, call your local **Goodwill** at (800) 664-6577. The recycling service of **IBM** will collect (and refurbish if needed) any computer; the cost is $29.99 for home pickup. Call 888-SHOP-IBM; use the reference number 06P7513.

➢ **Craft supplies:** To nursing homes or daycare centers.

➢ **Eyeglasses: The Lions Club** collects eyeglasses and sunglasses for needy people in developing countries. Drop off old pairs at a Lions Club center (800-74-SIGHT) or any Lens Crafters store.

➢ **Formals and Bridesmaid's dresses:** Several nonprofits around the country hand out formal dresses to teens who otherwise couldn't afford to attend the prom. You can mail your gowns to programs in Chicago (312-409-4139) Washington, D.C. (202-543-5298, ext. 106) or Dallas (214-319-3415); or drop them off at a designated boutique in your area. For a list, go to www.glassslipperproject.org.

➢ **Magazines:** Call local retirement homes to see if they are interested in your old magazines.

➢ **Paperback books:** Books to Prisoners will send books to inmates who request them. Mail paperbacks fourth class to:

1004 Turner Way E.,
Seattle, WA 98112
or call (206) 622-0195.

➢ **Stuffed animals/toys:**
Teddy Bears for Tikes (281-335-5434) gives used bears to children hurt in fires or whose homes have burned down. **Operation Toy Box** sends toys to disaster victims (114 White's Lane, Louisburg, NC 27549; 919-554-1410; optoybox@aol.com).

You can also contact local hospitals, police and fire stations, orphanages and homeless shelters, since they may provide stuffed animals to traumatized kids.

Refrigerator

Do you have foil-wrapped unknowns in your refrigerator? Most homes do. Here are some ways to keep the refrigerator looking good inside and out.

First, make it a habit to wipe up spills immediately before they dry. This is much easier. Then organize the shelves by grouping "like items" together. Put all the snack foods on one side of the shelf. Keep dairy products together. Have all the beverages on the door. Also store leftovers in one area of the refrigerator. Label your leftovers with an "eat by" date; that way, there will be no guessing needed a few days down the road. In addition line the vegetable and fruit bins with paper towels; they will absorb moisture and make for very easy clean up. And when you purchase chicken or meat from the store, place it on a plate to prevent the juices from leaking

Make sandwich-making a snap; place everything you commonly use to make a sandwich in a plastic bin. That way, you can pull out the bin and have everything you need without sorting through the shelves. There are also organizers made specifically for the inside of the refrigerator, like a soda can dispenser. It sits around the back of a shelf using wasted space and makes getting a soda easier. Whenever possible, use glass or clear-view plastic to store items; it's much easier to see what's inside.

Finally, keep things off the refrigerator. It shouldn't be a catchall for papers, photos and take out menus. And limit things like magnet collections on the refrigerator; the doors can become cluttered very easily.

Put juice in empty water bottles or spill-proof cups on the door so kids can get their own drinks without sticky spills.

Schedule

One sure way to cause chaos is to have more than one schedule or calendar for the household. If you write your appointments on one calendar and your children write theirs on another, you'll end up committing to be in two places at once. This, for obvious reasons, won't work.

It's important to have just one, and only one, family calendar. Everyone writes his or her appointments on that one calendar. When you get a flyer listing soccer games or dance practice, transcribe the dates onto the family calendar. This will alert you to scheduling conflicts immediately, and you can make alternate arrangements. An easy way to differentiate between children's activities is to have each child write in different color ink.

In addition plan activities for certain days. For example: Tuesday may be Laundry Night and everyone knows they need to have their laundry in the laundry room by 7 PM if they want it done that week. Thursday may be Errands Night. Run all your errands on one night instead of running out every night of the week. And Friday may be Family Night when the television gets turned off and you play games or do something as a family.

Have you ever had an experience like this? One of my client's arrived home from work to find her two children waiting by the front door. One had his soccer uniform on and reminded her that she needed to drive him and his friends to a game, which started at 4, and then stay to work the concession stand. Her other child was holding her trumpet and reminded her that she needed to be driven to practice that started at 4. What's a mother to do? She had marked her son's soccer game on her wall calendar and her daughters trumpet practice in her pocket calendar. This latest occasion of needing to be in two places at once caused her to rethink her time management system. She now has *one* place where she writes everything down. That way conflicts are realized immediately and can be dealt with.

Low on wall space where you could hang a family message board? Paint a cabinet door with blackboard paint (sold at most craft and hardware stores). Then attach cork· tiles to an adjoining cabinet or hang a wipe board.

Storage and Supplies

There are many types of storage containers available on the market today. There's a storage container made for just about every item that needs to be stored -- from rollaway carts, to under-the-bed flat storage, to gift-wrap storage containers. Take a look around your house to see what needs a storage container or what can be repackaged into an easier-to-use container.

While you're looking around the house, take a peek at what you're storing and ask yourself why. Is there something else that can be done with the stuff you've tucked away? Are there old clothes that can be donated or taken to a consignment shop? Are there books you have read that can be traded in for credit at a used bookstore or donated to a local nursing home? Take a long, hard look at what you're keeping.

If you are one of the millions that pay for a self-storage unit, think about whether or not it's worth it. What are you storing there? Do you ever need the items or can they be disposed of? Most of the time, you can unclutter areas of your home to make room for the items you want to continue to store. Then you can stop paying that monthly rental fee.

A great way to keep storage areas from becoming overcrowded is to place a "toss by" date on the box. If the box has not been opened and the contents used by the toss by date, then the box goes out. If you make this a rule, everyone in the house will get in the habit of dating and tossing their stored boxes, freeing up much needed space. The trick is to toss the box without opening it. Once you open it, you'll be reminded of what's in there and you'll not be as willing to part with it.

Keep all extra supplies on designated shelves or in specified cabinets or drawers. Collect all the extras you have and find a convenient place to keep them. For example: If you usually keep a lot of paper products on hand, then gather them up and find shelves where you can store them. Put napkins and paper towels on one shelf and toilet paper on another. Label the edges of the shelves so you know what goes where. That way you'll know what you're out of or someone else can help you by putting the items away. You'll know the supplies are going to the right places.

Don't drive yourself nuts trying to make changes to the way you do things in every room of the house. Take your time and implement a few new systems to a few rooms. Then evaluate how they work. Keep what works and modify what doesn't.

Chapter Highlights
- Pay attention to what you store and why.

- Keep your car clutter-free and up-to-date on maintenance.
- Containerize small items to keep them together.
- Have a desk stocked with necessary items.
- Prepare for disasters in advance.
- Consider pickup and delivery services instead of always running errands.
- Institute a family night and family meetings.
- Create a family notebook.
- Keep gifts and cards on hand.
- Do the laundry and the grocery shopping one time a week.
- Type up a morning checklist for your kids.
- Buy only easy-to-care-for clothes.
- Go through your mail one time a day beside a garbage can.
- Create a bill-paying caddy.
- Have a filing system in place.
- Stop answering the phone just because it rings.

Chapter Resources

- QVC.com 1-800-345-1515 – A shop from home channel that offers quality items for a fair price. QVC spotlights items that make your life easier. Ordering and returning are simple and their customer service is outstanding.
- rubbermaid.com
  1147 Akron Road
  Wooster, OH 44591-6000
  888-895-2110
- Mail away film place
- www.merrymaids.com - 1-800-we-serve
- www.netgrocer.com – 1-888-638-4762
- www.coolsavings.com – Print your own coupons for a wide variety of products and services
- www.goodwill.org -1-800-664-6577
- www.salvationarmy.org - 1-800-95-truck

- Books - Mail paperbacks fourth class to
  1004 Turner Way E.,
  Seattle, WA 98112
  or call (206) 622-0195
- www.dressforsuccess.org
- St Jude's Ranch PO Box 985 Boulder City Nevada
  89005
- National Cristina Foundation – 1(203) 863-9100
  www.cristina.org
- www.glassslipperproject.org – 312-409-4139
  email info@glassslipperproject.org
- The Lions Club (800-74-SIGHT) - Operation Toy
  www.operationtoybox.org - 919-554-1410
  Box 114 White's Lane
  Louisburg, NC 27549
- www.vermontteddybear.com
- www.pajamagram.com
- www.currentcatalog.com
- www.walmart.com
- www.drugstore.com
- www.petco.com
- www.1800flowers.com
- www.omahasteaks.com
- www.target.com
- www.tgbi.com - The Gift Basket - 781-642-1200
- www.sneakerland.com
- www.jellybelly.com
- www.muffinlady.com
- www.jockey.com
- www.autobarn.com
- www.bn.com
- www.amazon.com
- www.maids.com
- www.stamps.com - US Postal Service - 800-782-6724
- Life U Love – 1-866-294-9900
  369 Evergreen Blvd.
  Scotch Plains, NJ 07076
  www.lifeulove.com – jamie@lifeulove.com

Time Management and Priorities

This section is for you if:

- ➢ You have forgotten one or more appointments or anniversaries in the last 60 days.
- ➢ You procrastinate until the work or assignment becomes a panic situation.
- ➢ You waste valuable time waiting for appointments.
- ➢ You ate fast food for more than two meals this month.

Or if you answer, "yes" to any of the following:

- ➢ I usually run late or get there just in time.
- ➢ I often feel overwhelmed or rushed.
- ➢ I over-commit myself.
- ➢ There are times when I'm supposed to be in two places at once.
- ➢ I have missed one or more important family events in the last month.
- ➢ I seldom wear a watch.
- ➢ I sometimes wish I could just stop the world for a minute to breathe.

No matter what, you only get 24 hours in your day. Choose what you'll accomplish and let go of the rest.

Introduction

You're going to read about simple and easy-to-implement strategies for maximizing your time. Before we get to the strategies, let me share a story with you that I was forwarded to me. It came as an e-mail with no signature so I have no idea who wrote this. However I think it will hit home for many of you; it's called "A Thousand Marbles."

The older I get, the more I enjoy Saturday mornings. Perhaps it's the quiet solitude that comes with being the first to rise, or maybe it's the unbounded joy of not having to be at work. Either way, the first few hours of a Saturday morning are most enjoyable.

A few weeks ago, I was shuffling toward the basement shack with a steaming cup of coffee in one hand and the morning paper in the other. What began as a typical Saturday morning turned into one of those lessons that life seems to hand you from time to time.

Let me tell you about it. I turned the dial up into the phone portion of the band on my ham radio in order to listen to a Saturday morning swap net. Along the way, I came across an older sounding chap, with a tremendous signal and a golden voice. You know the kind, he sounded like he should be in the broadcasting business.

He was telling whomever he was talking with something about "a thousand marbles." I was intrigued and stopped to listen to what he had to say.

63

"Well, Tom, it sure sounds like you're busy with your job. I'm sure they pay you well, but it's a shame you have to be away from home and your family so much. Hard to believe a young fellow should have to work sixty or seventy hours a week to make ends meet. Too bad you missed your daughter's dance recital."

He continued, "Let me tell you something Tom, something that has helped me keep a good perspective on my own priorities." And that's when he began to explain his theory of a "thousand marbles."

"You see, I sat down one day and did a little arithmetic. The average person lives about seventy-five years. I know, some live more and some live less, but on average, folks live about seventy-five years."

"Now then, I multiplied seventy-five times fifty-two and I came up with thirty-nine hundred which is the number of Saturdays that the average person has in their entire lifetime. Now stick with me Tom, I'm getting to the important part. It took me until I was fifty-five years old to think about all this in any detail", he went on, "and by that time, I had lived through over twenty-eight hundred Saturdays. I got to thinking that if I lived to be seventy-five, I only had about a thousand of them left to enjoy."

"So I went to a toy store and bought every single marble they had. I ended up having to visit three toy stores to round up a thousand marbles. I took them home and put them inside of a large, clear plastic container right here in the shack next to my gear.

Every Saturday since then, I have taken one marble out and thrown it away. I found that by watching the marbles diminish, I focused more on the really important things in life. There is nothing like watching your time here on this earth run out to help get your priorities straight"

"Now let me tell you one last thing before I sign off with you and take my lovely wife out for breakfast. This morning, I took the very last marble out of the container. I figure if I make it until next Saturday then I have been given a little extra time. And the one thing we can all use is a little more time."

"It was nice to meet you Tom. I hope you spend more time with your family, and I hope to meet you again." You could have heard a pin drop on the radio when this fellow signed off.

I guess he gave us all a lot to think about. I had planned to work on the antenna that morning, and then I was going to meet up with a few hams to work on the next club newsletter. Instead, I went upstairs and woke my wife up with a kiss. "C'mon honey, I'm taking you and the kids to breakfast" "What brought this on?" she asked with a smile. "Oh, nothing special, it's just been a long time since we spent a Saturday together with the kids. Hey, can we stop at a toy store while we're out? I need to buy some marbles."

Hits home huh? You have the same amount of time each day as everyone else; it's what you do with that time that makes you different. Here are some time management skills that you can put into practice to get the most out of your 1,440 minutes every day. You're not going to read about how to cram more stuff into your already packed life. Time management is not about doing more stuff in less time; it's about getting the most important stuff done. In order to get the most important stuff done, you have to know what's important. Important stuff usually either has an unmovable deadline or is something you really care

65

about. If it's important, then make it a priority. It's good to know your top three priorities at all times. Make sure that what you're spending your time on agrees with your priorities. Take a moment and review your "to do" list. With each item, stop and ask yourself how important it is. You may cross some items off your list because although they may have been important when you first wrote them they're no longer crucial.

Please refer to the "To Do List" located in the back of the book.

Actually use a clock to determine how long tasks take you to complete. Once you know how long it takes you to get dressed, style your hair, eat breakfast and so on, you will never run late again. You will be able to calculate how long you need and you can start early enough, giving yourself plenty of time.

Learning to Set Limits
"No" is the single most important time management skill to learn. I know that when you're asked to do something, it can be difficult to say no. You will feel guilty if you say no. You want to be helpful so you say yes. Or you don't want to let someone down, so you say yes. Or you may just be in the habit of saying yes. Or you might say no and then wish later you had said yes. Or you may be afraid to miss an opportunity so you say yes. Before you say yes the next time think about this -- if you say yes, what are you really saying no to? For example, if you agree to attend a meeting, what are you saying no to? An evening with your family or a chance to go out with your spouse?

66

This is your life and your time. You are free to spend it any way you like. One of the best ways to ensure that you spend your time how you want is to wait twenty-four hours before agreeing to do something. When you're asked to do something, make sure you get the whole picture about what all will be involved before you agree to it. Then simply explain that you need twenty-four hours to talk it over with your spouse and/or family. The chances are very good that the person will either find someone else in the meantime or forget to call you back to get your answer.

If you're unable to say no but don't want to say yes, there's a great compromise. You can say yes while saying no. It works like this. Say someone asks you to make three-dozen cupcakes for the bake sale and you don't want to make time to bake them. Simply offer to make a cash donation instead. This accomplishes their fundraising goal and your goal of leaving your time free for things that you want to do. Note: there will be times when you cannot compromise so you actually have to decline outright.

Here are some ways to say no with a touch of grace:

Saying "No" Gracefully

I'm sorry, that's our family night.
I'm sorry, I just can't.
Thank you for thinking of me, but I can't.
Let me check my calendar and get back to you.
Thank you for asking me, but I just can't.
I'd love too, but I'm busy that day/night.
I've got other plans that day.
I've got something personal to attend to that day.
Normally I'd say yes, but I'm just overbooked right now.

Having a policy in place makes it easier to say no. You can refer back to your policy. Example: "I'm sorry but I only take on one volunteer project a year."

Commit this line to memory: "Let me check my calendar and get back to you."

Carry return address labels with you. That way when you have to write your information, you can simply stick on a label and save time.

Wear a watch and have clocks in every room. This allows you to keep an eye on the time and to measure how long tasks take you.

Time Saving Techniques
When you have to do something, it will save you time if you plan it out or think it through first. For example, writing out a shopping list prior to going to the store saves you time, money and energy. You can walk up and down the aisles picking up what you need and only what you need. You don't buy extras, you don't have to walk back for something you forgot, and you get done faster. Another tip for organized movement is to do "like things" together. If you're in the middle of cleaning, then continue on and clean another area. Don't stop to put clothes away. Another great timesaving tip is to shop at off-peak hours when the shelves are stocked and the lines are short. Yet another is to schedule the first appointment of the day, whether it's at your doctor's office, your hair salon, or wherever. Appointments tend to get behind as the day goes by.

A reader survey by *Home Office Computing Magazine* revealed that 43% of people struggle with managing time and 20% struggle with organization.

An excellent tip for saving time is to combine tasks. Can you listen to your child read their book report while you sort the laundry? Calling ahead also saves time. Many restaurants now offer "call-ahead seating." Note: combining tasks is different than multi-tasking. When you are combining tasks, you are taking two things that do not require your full attention and doing them simultaneously. Multi-tasking is when take two important tasks that each deserve your undivided attention and attempt to do them at the same time. Most times multi-tasking leads to stress and an unfinished or incorrectly done task. I don't recommend multi-tasking.

You could phone ahead of time to see if the store has what you need in stock. Call before an appointment to remind a person that you're coming. Also take advantage of pickup and delivery services. For example, I know some people who have their dry cleaning picked up and returned to them at work, and there is no extra change. What a time saver that is! Some stores, like office supply stores, will deliver your order right to your doorstep. In addition if you have a commute to work, use this time wisely. You can listen to books on tape if you're driving or get work or leisure reading done if you take a train. Another idea is to join or start a car pool in your neighborhood to avoid having to drive your children both ways everywhere they need to go. You can alternate turns driving to and from school, the mall, dances, the movies, practices and more.

A survey by Day-Timers Inc. found that the average American worker spends 35 minutes commuting to work.

Below you'll find a short list of examples of tasks that can be done in five minutes or less. Add to this one or create your own list and hang it up some place handy. When you find yourself with a few minutes to spare consider doing something on your list.

Catching Up in Your Spare Time

> Run a dust cloth over an area.
> Weed through a Rolodex.
> Return a call.
> Make an appointment.
> Call to see if a store has what you need in stock.
> Iron something.
> Sign children's homework and permission slips.
> Choose your outfit for the morning.
> Toss old food from the refrigerator.
> Put in a load of laundry.
> Sit and relax.
> Swish the toilet.
> Clean the kitchen sink.
> Hang up an outfit.
> De-clutter an area.
> Read your children a story.
> Care for a pet.
> Delete old files off the computer.

Use Your "Prime Time" Well

Do you know what time of day is your "prime time"? Prime time refers to the hours of the day when you're at your best. This is when your mind is the sharpest and you have the most patience and ability to handle challenging tasks. Some people are at their best in the morning hours, before the day takes over. Other people find themselves full of energy and ready to go later on in the day. Pay attention to how you feel throughout the day. Are you a morning, afternoon or night person? Knowing the answer will help you; you can plan to do the tasks that take the most out of you during your prime time.

The Value of Time

To realize the value of ONE YEAR, ask a student who failed a grade.

To realize the value of ONE MONTH, ask a mother who gave birth to a premature baby.

To realize the value of ONE WEEK, ask the editor of a weekly newspaper.

To realize the value of ONE HOUR, ask the lovers who are waiting to meet.

To realize the value of ONE MINUTE, ask a person who missed the train.

To realize the value of ONE SECOND, ask a person who just avoided an accident.

Treasure every moment! Yesterday is history. Tomorrow is a mystery. Today is a gift.

That's why it's called the present!

Prepare the Night Before

Here's a great idea to eliminate those hectic mornings -- the ones where you have to hunt for your car keys and then you try to make a mad dash to your job but get behind drivers going 10 miles per hour! *Get ready for your day the night before.* Choose your outfit and lay out all the pieces including the accessories. Have the kids pick out their clothes too. Watch the weather so you'll know if you need an umbrella or have to wake up early to shovel the walkway. Designate one location where you'll place everything that you need to take with you, like your purse and briefcase; the kids can do the same thing with their backpacks. Make the lunches or hand out lunch money the night before and make sure you sign all papers and that homework is complete. You can even go so far as to fill the coffee pot with coffee and water and set the table for breakfast.

Stagger kids' wake-up times by 10 minutes so you can get one ready or at least started first.

Print out labels for addresses you commonly use so you can avoid writing the same information over and over.

Turn off the television and log off the computer. Stop surfing the web and playing video games.

According to Nielsen Media Research, the average American watches twenty-eight hours of television per week. And by the time we are sixty-five most people have spent nine years watching television!

Shun the Telemarketers

One of the most common and most disliked of all the interruptions is the telemarketer call. There's an easy way to put an end to these annoying calls. Simply write your name and telephone number on a piece of paper and mail it to the following address. They will delete your name from the calling lists. The address is:

Direct Marketing Association
Telephone Preference Service
P.O. Box 9008
Farmingdale, NY 11735-9008.

Or you can purchase one of the new telezapper devices on the market today. When a call comes in that originated from a computer-dialed phone, the machine clicks on and repeats a pre-recoded message stating that this number does not accept telemarketing calls. The machine then asks the caller to remove your number from their database.

Kids don't need to be signed up for dance, swim and horseback riding lessons at the same time, or soccer and softball in the same season. Make it a rule; one or two activities a season.

The Problem of Procrastination
Procrastination is a huge time-waster. There are things you should be doing but for one reason or another you're putting them off. Here are the most common thoughts that cause procrastination and ways you can reverse your thinking.

Old thought:	I'll do it when I'm in the mood
New thought:	Do it now, do it right, do it once.

Old thought:	I'll start tomorrow.
New thought:	There is no time like the present.

Old thought:	There's plenty of time to get it done.
New thought:	If I do it now, I won't have to think about it any more.

Old thought:	I don't know where to begin.
New thought:	I'll start here.

Old thought:	I work better under pressure.
New thought:	I can relax if I get it done and over with right now.

Old thought:	It will not turn out perfect, so why start.
New thought:	I'll do my best and be satisfied with the results.

Old thought:	I enjoy the rush of the last minute.
New thought:	Too many things around me cause my adrenaline to surge.

Old thought:	I'm fearful of how it will turn out.
New thought:	I'll take small steps towards getting it done.

Old thought:	I don't want to do it.
New thought:	Once I get it over and done with, I won't have to think about it any longer.

Old thought:	I'm too busy to do it.
New thought:	I'll make the time to get it done.

Old thought:	I should do this.
New thought:	I choose to do this.

One way to combat procrastination is to just start whatever it is you want to do but are delaying. You cannot finish until you start. In addition give yourself a deadline; self-imposed deadlines work well to get the ball rolling. Still can't get going? How about if you do the worst thing first thing in the morning? That way no matter what you do the rest of the day; nothing will be as bad. Setting a timer and doing as much of a task as you can in X number of minutes also can be very helpful in breaking through procrastination. And most times once you get started it's easy to keep going. You can reward yourself too; for me, a piece of chocolate works every time. I simply agree that once I get X done, I'll have my reward. You can always take small steps toward accomplishing your goal. You can do anything for fifteen minutes; so agree to do it for just a quarter of an hour, often you'll find that you'll just stick with it longer. And when all else fails, just do it despite everything. You'll be surprised how much you can get done when you just decide to do it no matter what.

 Do it now, do it well, do it once.

Don't give out your cell phone number or have it printed on your business card. Only family members should have the number in case of an emergency. Your cell phone should be used at your convenience to retrieve voice mail messages or to return calls.

"It takes less time to do things right than to explain why you did it wrong." Henry Wadsworth Longfellow

Finding More Time
We've looked at ways to manage your time and overcome procrastination. But what about when you simply need more time?

Take a look at these statistics.

Waking up one hour earlier every day for a year will give you almost ten extra weeks!

Turning off the television for one hour a week will give you fifty-two hours a year!

Working with an Organizer
The first and most important step to self-management is to come up with a way to keep track of your appointments and

schedule. Most people find an organizer works best. The question then becomes what type of organizer. There's a wide variety of organizers on the market, ranging from the electronic handheld type to paper organizers. Neither option is particularly better than the other; they just work differently. You need to pick the one that works best for you.

So the question really is how do you work? Are you more comfortable with a pen or a keypad? Here are some things to consider when making the decision between paper and electronic organizers. Do you write better then you type? Do you like to flip back and forth between pages in your planner? Do you lie to get an overview of your day, week or month? Can you remember on what paper or where on a paper you wrote something down? How do you write your "to do" list? Do you list calls to make, things to buy and things to do rather then having them all one list? Then choose the paper organizer. You will have a choice of views, there are daily, weekly and monthly views available. Remember if it is too complicated you will not use it, so go with simple. It may have a nice outer cover; it could feature a zipper, snap, or Velcro or perhaps not have a way to close it. Page size varies too, how large do you like your pages? And look at the paper designs available; you'll find everything from nature scenes to motivational quotes. Watch that the paper design is not bold enough to interfere if you write in pencil.

However you'll probably want an electronic organizer if you generally remember appointments by the date, day of the week, and/or the time of day. Can you look at a screen representing a part of the day or week and view the whole week or month? Do your thoughts flow more easily with fingers on the keyboard rather than pen on paper? How is your "to do" list organized? Do you list your "to dos" in order of priority? Then the computerized organizer is the best choice for you. There are a wide variety of electronic organizers in the marketplace. Talk to someone in your type of business who uses one to get practical suggestions and ideas from those who actually use electronic organizers and don't just sell them. '

A few things to keep in mind if you choose electronic:

1. Save your changes as you go.
2. Back up to disk.
3. Watch for low-battery level.
4. Synchronize with your desktop computer at least once a day.

There's no one perfect organizing tool, the key is just to choose one and stick with it. Having more than one place to record your activities leads to over scheduling and double booking. Keep in mind that there is no one perfect way. The key is to pick one that is right for you and stick with it. Note: Having more than one place to record your activities leads to over-scheduling and double booking.

Once you choose the organizer that's right for you, it's important to use it correctly. This means having the organizer with you almost everywhere you go. Once again, my advice is to use only one organizer; transcribing appointments from others onto the main one. One way you might use an organizer is to record the dates of your child's soccer games, the meetings at church, etc. If you have chosen an electronic organizer, it will allow you to enter reoccurring events and reminders. With either method you can use color or a different appearance to distinguish different types of items in your organizer. For example, all items in blue could be for your child and red items might be urgent.

Be sure to leave time around appointments; do not schedule them back-to-back. This allows for prep time and breathing room. Plus you don't have to make anyone wait if your first appointment runs over. Take a look at your calendar and make sure that there's some blank space. Schedule time for yourself before you start filling in other appointments; if you don't make a point of noting this, it will not be there later. And schedule reading time, planning time and filing time.

E-mail to phone, Internet on phone, pictures to phone. Do you really need these options? You lived without them before.

More Time Management Basics
Once you've chosen a way to keep track of things, you need to do more work with your time management. It's good to calculate how much your time is really worth. For example, if you make $50,000 a year that breaks down to about $24 an hour. So now you have a better idea of what it costs monetarily for you to do a task; this does not take into account what it costs you in other ways – like stress and aggravation. Those aspects are why we talk about things like delegation and hiring out projects. If someone else has the resources to do the job quicker, cheaper and with less aggravation, it may be worth considering giving that project to them to do. But you can't hire out or delegate all the tasks; there will always be something for you to do. That's where some of the following self-management ideas come into play.

First off, take out your organizer and schedule time for yourself. Are you in need of a haircut? Do you want to set time aside to do a school project with one of your children? Would you and your spouse like to have an evening out alone together, just the two of you? Put all these things into the organizer first. Also, try to include small steps towards a few of those "I'll get around to them sometime" dreams you have. Keep a list in your organizer and, as time permits, add them into your schedule. Perhaps you have always wanted to take a second honeymoon; there's no time like the present to get plans underway. Maybe start a savings account and visit a travel agent to get brochures on places to visit.

You also need some undevoted time to work on things that pop up or to just give yourself time to breathe. Things always come up so it's not a good idea to schedule things from the beginning to the end of the day. You need free time to catch up, to simply read a little, or to brainstorm on new ideas; these are things that cannot be easily scheduled.

After you have planned, actually block out time to work on a project that's coming due or that filing you've been meaning to tackle. By scheduling routine tasks, there's a greater probability that you'll have time to get them done.

What About Project Management?
Let's look now at some ideas about project management. Before you begin a project, check to make sure you have all the necessary pieces to finish it. There's nothing worse than getting into the middle of a job and realizing that you need to run out and buy something. Once you start the project try your best to keep from getting distracted or interrupted. There are a few tricks. Don't have your desk facing the door; this discourages unwelcome visitors from stopping in to chat. Also, if you remember something you need to do while you're working, jot it down instead of switching tasks. It may seem harmless enough to stop your work just to type a quick e-mail, but that's never the case. You open the e-mail to compose a letter and now see that you have messages. Next thing you know you are reading incoming e-mails and dealing with those issues and have abandoned your original project.

An hour of planning can save you up to ten hours of doing.

To keep papers related to separate projects from mixing together, give each project its own folder. Place the name of the project on the folder and use the same name for the project files in the computer. Next, give each project a deadline -- even if it's a self-imposed one. Then the trick is to put away projects even if they're only half-done. For instance don't leave a report sprawled across your desk when you go to attend a scheduled meeting. Though you may have every intension of getting right back to it this will probably not happen. So place the report in the project file and put the file away before the meeting. If it's important enough you won't forget to go back to the project. Anyway it's on your "to do" list, isn't it?

Using a timer during tasks goes a long way to helping you stay on track. You're much more aware of time if a clock is ticking down. Tasks will usually expand to fill the amount of time you've allotted for them. If you have a five-page report to write and you have all day it will probably take you that long. And if you have just the morning it will probably take you that amount of time. Give yourself deadlines to work within.

Clutter-Busting Your Purse or Wallet
Another part of self-management is getting a handle on the clutter in your wallet or purse. It's common for people to carry business cards in their wallets. They take up a lot of space and are unnecessary. Take all the business cards out of your wallet daily and enter the contact information into your contact database. Get into a habit of emptying your wallet or purse every time you come home. It will only take a few minutes. This is much easier to do daily, than to have to spend hours sorting through papers whenever you get around to it. Carry only the essentials. For a day or two,

notice what you really use. And what are you toting around that you don't use or could easily get? Also, take a look at the credit and other cards that you carry. Do you have more than one credit card? Do you stuff your wallet with tons of family pictures? Consider carrying cash, one credit card, your insurance card, your auto club card and one or two recent family photos.

What a Wallet Isn't

It's not a:
> ➤ Date book; instead use your calendar.
> ➤ Rolodex, instead enter business cards into your contact manager.
> ➤ Catchall for movie ticket stubs and other memorabilia instead use a scrapbook.
> ➤ Filing cabinet for receipts instead use a real filing cabinet.
> ➤ Bank for tons of loose change; instead toss change into a coin machine or save it for a rainy day.
> ➤ Photo album; instead carry only a few recent photos

I once worked with a client who carried a huge black bag with her everywhere she went. She had it stuffed so full that the zipper had broken. The client explained that this was actually for the best because now she could shove even more stuff in! One day I asked her what would happen if she ever lost the bag. "I'd just die!" she exclaimed. "Wow, that must put a lot of stress on you, to have to always know where your bag is." I responded. She thought for a moment and then agreed with me. Her big, black bag which was supposed to make her life easier by holding everything she might need, was actually causing her stress. Together we sorted through the bag to see what was so important.

Here is a list of what we found inside:

• Three open packs of tissues	• Receipts
• Two wallets	• Her own business cards
• A coin purse	• Others' business cards
• Loose change	• Bills
• A mini first aid kit	• Unopened mail
• A toothbrush and toothpaste	• Pens (some worked, some didn't)
• A cell phone and charger	• Nail polish
• Hand lotion	• Loose makeup
• Checks and a check register	• A nail file
• An organizer	• A calculator
• A calendar	• Nail clippers
• "To do" lists on loose papers	• Chapstick
• An overdue library book	• A brush
• An overdue movie rental	• Batteries
• Mints	• Scrunchies
• Several packs of gum	• Car keys
• Candy	• House keys
• Rolls of undeveloped film	• A spare set of her keys
• An envelope of developed pictures	• Reading glasses
	• Sunglasses
	• A bottle of aspirin
	• A mini sewing kit
	• Bottle of vitamins

Sounds like that magical carpetbag Mary Poppins had, doesn't it? But my client actually did have all this; she just kept pulling stuff out of that black bag. We looked at each item and held it up. Each time, I asked, "What's the worst thing that could happen if you didn't have this with you?"

Here's how it went and what she decided to do about carrying around each of the items.

OLD WAY	NEW WAY
Three open packs of tissues	Carry one

OLD WAY	NEW WAY
Two wallets	Combine items. Carry one wallet with the essentials
Coin purse	Take it out, you don't use it anyway
Loose change	Leave it on the bottom of the purse until the night she takes it out and puts it in the money jar by the front door
Mini first aid kit	Stashed two Band-Aids in her wallet
Toothbrush and toothpaste	Put those in her desk drawer at work to use after lunch
Cell phone and charger	Kept cell phone; left the charger at home to use at night
Hand lotion	Bought a mini-bottle to carry
Checks and check register	Left these at home in her newly created bill-paying caddy
Organizer	Cleaned out old papers and kept it
Calendar	Tossed; decided to use the one in her organizer
To-do lists on loose papers	Bought a small spiral notebook and transcribed all the loose papers
Overdue library book	Placed in an errands bag in her car
Overdue movie rental	Placed in an errands bag in her car
Mints	Kept
Gum	Kept one pack
Candy	Tossed
Rolls of undeveloped film	Mailed to film developing company

OLD WAY	NEW WAY
Envelope of developed pictures	Put these in a photo box at home for the next time she had a photo night and pasted the pictures into scrapbooks
Receipts	Placed them all in an envelope she will change every month
Own business cards	Kept a few; will refill carrier when it's close to empty
Others' business cards	Took them out and put them in an envelope to enter into her contact database
Bills	Took them all out and put them in the bill-paying caddy
Unopened mail	Sorted it, tossed junk and put bills in the bill-paying caddy
Pens (some worked, some didn't)	Kept two good working pens
Nail polish	Took it out and put this in the nail-polishing caddy at home
Loose makeup	Kept a few essentials and placed them in a make-up bag
Nail file	Placed it in the make-up bag
Calculator	Put it in the bill-paying caddy
Nail clippers	Put it in the make-up bag
Chapstick	Put it in the make-up bag

OLD WAY	NEW WAY
Brush	Put it in the make-up bag
Batteries	Put them away at home
Scrunchies	Kept one in her make-up bag
Car keys	Kept these but combined them with the house keys; took off the unknown keys
House keys	Kept these but combined them with the car keys; took off unknown keys
Spare keys	Placed them in a magnetic hide-a-key holder under her car's bumper
Reading glasses	Kept
Sunglasses	Kept these in her car
Bottle of aspirin	Took out two and placed them in a small pill container
Mini sewing kit	Kept a safety pin attached to her make-up bag and tossed the rest
Bottle of vitamins	Kept a weeks worth in the small pill container with the aspirin

Boy, did her life change; she felt so much freer. Now she could concentrate on other things rather than keeping an eye on her bag. This client now travels with a sleek, black purse and loves it. She has yet to run into a situation where she needed something she had tossed out of her bag and couldn't find it somewhere.

Tackling the "To Do" List
When you wake up, do you have grand plans for what you're going to get done that day? But by the end of the day, you have actually accomplished very little -- or at least it feels that way? Wouldn't it be a great feeling to reach the

85

end of your day and have each item on your "to do" list checked off? What a sense of accomplishment! Well, it *is* possible. How you ask. By simply gaining an understanding of the three, yes three, types of "to do" lists. When you're using them in a way that works for you, you'll have your daily tasks checked off by bedtime.

You need to reevaluate your "to do" list if any of the following apply:

➤ You don't have a list.
➤ Your list is in your head.
➤ You just saw your list a minute ago; hang on, you'll find it there somewhere.
➤ Your list is so long it would take you days to write it all down.

First, there's the traditional, daily "to do" list. This list consists only of the 5 to 10 tasks that you actually intend on accomplishing that day before you go to bed. The first trick is to keep this "to do" list realistic. We each only have so many hours in the day. Just writing a task on the list does not ensure there is actually going to be time to get to it. To accomplish all you set out to do, be reasonable. Items like picking up the kids from daycare and calling to make a doctors' appointment are perfect examples of what belongs on this daily "to do" list.

You need to prioritize your daily "to do" list in a way that works for you. You can give each item a letter, A, B or C, or a number, 1, 2, or 3. A or 1 would be the most important task, and C or 3, the least important. Or you can simply group your "to do" list items by categories: to call, to buy and more.

For you perfectionists, rewriting your "to do" list so it's neat.

Before adding an item to your daily "to do" list, ask yourself, "Does this need to be done?" And if so, also ask, "Does this need to be done by me?" The answer to both may be yes. But in some cases, you'll be able to simplify the task, delegate it, hire it out or perhaps even skip the task completely. And remember: The unexpected sometimes happens and you may not get to everything on your list. That's okay; you're human. Praise yourself for what you did get done instead of beating yourself up about what you didn't.

"Focus on the critical few, not the insignificant many...even the most powerful waves begin as a single drop." Author Unknown

One last thought on your daily "to do" list; keep the list handy. You won't be able to cross off completed items or add new ones if you can't find your list. It's helpful to have your "to do" list be the first page in your organizer, or you may choose to have your list on a separate pad. A spiral one works well, you won't lose pages. Or if you're using an electronic organizer, you may choose to keep your "to do" list there.

"I write down everything I want to remember. That way, instead of spending a lot of time trying to remember what it is I wrote down, I spend the time looking for the paper I wrote it down on." Beryl Pfizer

The second type is the "wish I had time to do" list. This is a running list of all the things you want to get to eventually. This wish "to do" list usually includes tasks like clean the gutters, hem a skirt, get together with a friend for coffee, and so on. Everything that comes to mind -- from a vacation in Florida to landscaping the front yard -- belongs on your wish "to do" list.

"Look at a day when you're supremely satisfied at the end. It's not a day when you lounge around doing nothing; it's when you've had everything to do, and you've done it." Margaret Thatcher

These tasks should get added to your daily "to do" list on the day you actually plan to do them. It makes no sense to have daily tasks and wish to do tasks on the same list, you will never have enough time in one day to get to them all. You'd just be setting yourself up to fail. You might as well set yourself up for success by keeping two lists and learning how to manage them.

A great way to move closer to accomplishing a large item on the second list is to break it up into smaller more doable tasks. Say you'd like to take a trip to Florida; you might open a vacation bank account and that task would go on the daily "to do" list the day you actually plan to do it. The trip would be on your wish "to do" list.

Then there is the third and last list, which is usually the most popular of the three. It's the "not to do" list. This list usually has such "not to do" tasks as:

> Don't answer the phone but let the machine screen the calls
> Don't make the bed everyday; let it breathe once in awhile.
> Don't watch the news; it's energy draining and sucks up valuable time.

This list is where you place all those tasks that you have decided you'll no longer be doing. You may choose to not answer the phone or at least not during dinnertime. You may decide to no longer say yes to any meetings or events that take place on Thursday nights, because that night has been designated family game night. By writing down what you have made a pact with yourself not to do, you're more apt to stick to your decision.

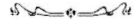

Try to get a handle on a few time management techniques. By simply making a few adjustments to how you do things, you'll find "spare" time in your day. And always remember that this is *your* life and *your* time to spend how *you* want.

Chapter Highlights
- Say "no" more often with grace.
- Get ready for the day the night before.
- Eliminate interruptions.
- Overcome procrastination.
- Turn off the television and log off the computer.
- Use some sort of a calendar/organizer system.

- Know how much your time is worth.
- Schedule all activities.
- Leave room for the unexpected.
- Use a timer when working on projects.
- Have everything you need to finish before starting a project.
- Put projects in their own folders.
- File projects away when not in use.
- Write your daily "to do" list down on paper.
- Know the difference between the three types of "to do" lists.
- Prioritize your lists.
- Keep your lists handy.

Chapter Resources
- ACT Contact Database - www.act.com
- PDA's – Personal Digital Assistant
- www.daytimer.com - 800-225-5005
- www.franklincovey.com - 1-800-819-1812
- Life U Love – 1-866-294-9900
  369 Evergreen Blvd.
  Scotch Plains, NJ 07076
  www.lifeulove.com – jamie@lifeulove.com

**After that, start putting yourself first, without neglecting anyone else.
AKA Self care and nurturing**

This section is for you if:
- You have a difficult time getting out of bed in the morning.
- You feel that you have lost touch with who you are.
- You are overdue for a dentist and/or doctor appointment.

Or if you answer, "yes" to any of the following:
- I resent spending my time on others needs while I disregard my own.
- I have no unscheduled free time.
- I feel tired most days.
- Whenever I spend time on something for myself, I feel guilty.
- I have been ill more than twice in the past six months.
- I could be in better physical condition and/or eat healthier.

91

Introduction

Self-care not selfish; these are two different things. Self-care is acknowledging that you have needs and that they *do* matter. For those of you not accustomed to taking excellent care of yourself, it may seem selfish at first. But trust me, that feeling will fade in time and you'll come to rely on your self-care practices to renew your energy and spirit. Taking excellent care of yourself allows you to be a better spouse, parent, friend, employee and an all around better person.

First off, it's necessary for you to schedule a minimum of ten uninterrupted minutes each and every day. During this time do something just for yourself. Here are some good suggestions of how to use this time:

➢ Give yourself or get a manicure or pedicure. ➢ Get a facial. ➢ Take a nap. ➢ Start or get back to a hobby. ➢ Take a bath or an extra long shower. ➢ Sit and be quiet.	➢ Take a walk. ➢ Listen to comedy tapes and laugh. ➢ Read something enjoyable. ➢ Take a class. ➢ Get a massage. ➢ Play with a pet.

These are only a few suggestions. Start with one of them or come up with your own. Notice that the list makes no mention of things like cooking, vacuuming, or watching television, as these are not examples of reenergizing tasks. The whole goal is to spend the time nurturing *you*.

Qualities of a Balanced Person

➢ Acknowledge that you can't do it all! ➢ Accept that you'll never be done.	➢ Know your priorities and remain flexible as priorities change.

➢ Believe that relationships mean more than a clean house, a three-course dinner, spotless laundry or being a size "6." ➢ Write your goals down and work towards them each and every day. ➢ Recognize that you have needs and become comfortable with fulfilling them.	➢ Stop striving for perfection, accept and be okay with imperfection. ➢ Determine and stick to your limits and boundaries. ➢ Get good at saying "no" gracefully. ➢ Give up your pursuit of being a "super woman." ➢ Remember that being balanced is an ongoing journey, not a destination.

Your needs have to be met and you have to give yourself time to reenergize, otherwise you will have very little left to give to others.

I once worked with a client who gave new meaning to the word "giving." She gave her time and energy to every person and cause that demanded it of her. She had three, young, children, a husband who traveled often for business, was on multiple committees and much more. She had been to many of my lectures where I touted the benefits of self-care. She listened but never took my advice. I often spoke with her personally after presentations when she would run down a list of all the current activities that required her time. Even before she finished the list, I was tired. During one of our last talks, I challenged her. I asked her to do one thing just for her. She laughed. I told her I was serious; I really wanted her to take twenty minutes just for her. "But what will I do?" she asked. We discussed some possibilities and she decided to take twenty minutes to soak in a tub. To ensure that she would be left alone she decided to wait until her husband would be home so he could be in charge of the children. And she even posted a note on the bathroom door reminding the family that she was have quiet time from 7 to 7:20. Then she took a luxurious bath. She called me that evening to let me know how it went. She explained that at first she felt really guilty. She just sat there thinking of all the things she thought she should be doing. Laundry, returning phone calls, dishes, the list went on and on. But once she let go of those feelings she was able to relax and enjoy her quiet time. One her bath was over she was relaxed and actually had more energy. She was amazed! She had the patience and desire to get a few more things done before bed that night. She felt better and she now relies on her self-care rituals to renew her energy and spirit.

In the beginning, it may be difficult for the people around you to get used to your alone time. To help family members remember, you may find it helpful to hang a sign on the door.

| *Quiet Please*

Mommy is having her "alone time" until 5 o'clock

Thank you | *Daddy is having quiet time.*

Please go to Mommy if you need something. |

 Make an appointment with yourself and keep it.

Children laugh an average of 400 times a day. Adults only average 20 times.

Be a Kid Again!
- ➤ Goof off.
- ➤ Walk barefoot in the grass or sand.
- ➤ Swing or seesaw or run really fast.
- ➤ Paint or color; you don't have to stay in the lines.
- ➤ Mold clay or mud pies.
- ➤ Dance like no one is watching.
- ➤ Smile and let your teeth show.
- ➤ Sing out loud even if you don't know all the words.
- ➤ Play like you have no cares in the world.

Go to an amusement park with a friend or spouse. Ride the rides, visit the arcades or play a round of miniature golf.

"Do not take life too seriously. You'll never get out alive." Elbert Hubbard

The Power of Journaling
Journaling is another great way to take care of yourself. The numerous documented benefits include stress relief, problem-solving and venting. There are many ways to journal but the most popular approach is "free-writing." With this technique, you simply recount your day. Write about what's bothering you or what's going well.

A study of asthma and arthritis sufferers found that those who wrote for twenty minutes a day on three

95

consecutive days about their most stressful events showed significant improvements in their health.

So write in your journal for three consecutive days (at least twenty minutes each time) to gain some great benefits. Journal during your lunch break, or just before sleeping. Or you could wake up a little earlier every morning this will help you find time to fit it into your schedule.

When choosing a journal, keep in mind that there's no one perfect kind. You may be drawn to an ornate journal covered in jewels or a simple spiral-bound notebook may make you feel more comfortable. The choice is yours. Let your journal reflect you. Remember, no one journal is permanent; try one out and you can always choose a different one next time.

Aside from journaling about your day and things that happen, you can journal about things that you're grateful for. Commonly called a "gratitude journal" you would make simply lists. Then as you spend time rereading the journal, you will realize how truly lucky you are.

Please refer to the Journaling Prompts located in the back of the book.

```
┌─────────────────────────────────────────────┐
│        Things to Be Grateful for Right Now   │
│                                               │
│  Think of how grateful you are for the       │
│  following:                                   │
│  Your family                                  │
│  Your friends                                 │
│  Your job                                     │
│  Your health                                  │
│  Start a list of your own and add five items │
│  to it each day. When you are feeling down    │
│  read the list.                               │
│                                               │
└─────────────────────────────────────────────┘
```

Try a specialty journal. Types of specialty journals include gardening, vacation, holiday, pregnancy/baby, and hobby journals -- just to name a few.

Doing Away with "Tolerations"

Being kind to yourself also includes eliminating what I refer to as "tolerations." Tolerations are things that can hold you back, cause you grief, waste your time, take your energy, sidetrack you, and make you feel bad. In addition, they keep you from living in the moment. To be able to eliminate them, you first have to know what they are. To identify yours, make a list, writing down everything you can think of that you're tolerating. I often hear people mention such things as stacks of clutter, being out of shape, broken appliances, an ex-spouses' items still lying around, how poorly someone treats them, or an out-of-date room in the house, especially the bathroom or kitchen.

Once you have identified your tolerations your next move is easy. You work on eliminating them. Some tolerations can be eliminated in one step; others will require multiple steps. Here's a multi-step example: If you listed "being out of shape" as something that you're tolerating, you'd start taking steps towards becoming healthier. You might toss out the junk food from your kitchen cabinets, then buy

97

fresh fruits and vegetables. You might spend some time preparing healthy meals and freezing them so you can heat them up on a busy night instead of running by a fast-food drive-up window. And there are many other things you can do to work towards maintaining a healthier lifestyle. Once you start to take action to eliminate something you're tolerating you immediately begin to feel better.

You Don't Have to Do Everything
Another part of self-care is starting to realize that everything doesn't depend on you. Although sometimes it may feel that it does, trust me. Things would carry on and people would get things done if you weren't around. So stop trying to solve everything and your life will become much easier. Another part of that is learning to ask for help when you need it or to accept it when assistance is offered. You probably like the feeling you get when someone thanks you for helping him or her; allow others to have that same feeling by letting him or her to help you!

Try Some Stress-Busting
Similar to eliminating "tolerances" is trying to minimize stress. The first step is identifying what stresses you out. You may often find yourself with half-finished projects on the day they're due or have a very difficult commute. Take a good look around and notice what stresses you. Then take steps to cut out the stressors. This may be as simple as delegating some tasks to get a project done on time. Or you may want to look at alternate routes to work.

Ways to Combat the Stress in Your Life
There are many ways to combat stress. Here are some important ones:

> ➤ Eat well-balanced meals and take multivitamins.
> ➤ Get seven to nine hours of sleep a night.
> ➤ Limit your caffeine and sugar intake.

- ➤ Exercise for at least twenty minutes a day most days.
- ➤ Journal about your stress for at least twenty minutes a day three days a week.
- ➤ Use your creativity; paint, sing, or dance away your stress.
- ➤ Talk it over with trusted friend or a qualified professional.

Really stop and experience how it feels when someone says thank you to you or compliments you. Pay attention to how it feels to be appreciated. Acknowledge that you did do something instead of quickly brushing it off.

"There is an important difference between giving up and letting go." Jessica Hatchigan

Ask for What You Want

You also have to remember that people are not mind readers; they cannot be expected to know what you want unless you tell them. Imagine walking up to a coffee shop counter and standing there. It would be silly to think that the clerk will know what type of latte to fix for you. So you must learn to ask for what you want. If you're not used to that, it may feel a little uncomfortable at first. Try it out and soon you'll be getting exactly what you want. It's amazing what can happen when you ask for what you want.

After one of my more recent lectures I was approached by a woman who told me that she never got what she wanted. I thought this was strange; she had to get what she wanted at least some of the time. So we talked for a little bit. I asked her to give me an example of a time when she did not get what she wanted. She proceeded to tell me a story of a day when she had a taste for Chinese food. She really enjoyed the house dish from a local restaurant and she was hoping all day that her and her husband could eat out that night. She called him at work and suggested eating out. He agreed and asked where she would like to go. Her response was, "Anywhere, you pick." Then she hoped that he would pick the Chinese restaurant. But he didn't, he chose Italian. She was disappointed but agreed and that night they ate Italian food. When we took a closer look at how she had approached getting her needs met we found that she had done a good job with the first part. By calling her husband and expressing her wish to eat out half of her need was met. However for some reason when she was asked what she wanted she reverted to her habit of automatically answering it does not matter what I want we'll get what you want. This is where she was failing herself; she had the opportunity to state her wish but didn't. She we decided she had some work to do. We actually practiced having her state her needs, wishes and desires. I asked her, what movie would you like to see? What would you like for dinner? What would you like to do tonight and so on. At first her automatic response was to ask me what I wanted. I stopped her and she was able to regroup and say what she wanted. It took a few weeks of practice, but soon she found herself getting what she wanted a good portion of the time, and loving it.

Stand by Your Boundaries
Another key self-care practice to put in place is setting and sticking by your boundaries. Most of us don't often think about boundaries so this one may take a little work. But once you get it and you start sticking to your boundaries, your life will be much more enjoyable. The idea behind boundaries is to decide what you are and what you are *not* willing to put up with, tolerate or accept. Determine what your boundaries are and start living by them. Once you

teach people how you like to be treated you'll start getting treated the way you like. It's great how it all works out.

Eating and Living Healthy
Self-care also includes taking care of your health and nutritional needs. That means being up-to-date with all your doctor appointments. Maintaining your cholesterol and blood pressure within acceptable limits. Keeping your weight in the ideal range. Keeping your teeth and gums healthy and seeing your dentist regularly. Eating healthy, and taking your vitamins and any prescription medications as directed. Not abusing alcohol, not smoking, and watching your intake of caffeine and sugar from such items as coffee, soda, candy and junk foods. Also monitor your consumption of comfort foods-- cakes, ice cream, etc. -- that you reach for to fill you. Exercising, drinking plenty of water, and not using illegal drugs are all important to your overall health. Getting enough sleep is another important factor. You can be really indulgent and go to bed by 9:00 PM one night a week; you'll be amazed by the difference it makes. Be sure to pay attention to your body and how it feels. You know your body better than anyone.

Beware of eating while doing another activity, such as watching television. It's important to concentrate while eating. You'll notice the food, the flavor, the texture and the taste. You'll also be aware of the food filling you up. This is called "mindful eating."

Nutrition Suggestions

➢ Here's some tips for eating in a healthy way:
➢ Eat plenty of fresh fruits or vegetables daily.
➢ Eat a wide variety of foods and eat them in their natural state. Eat some raw fruits and vegetables every day.
➢ Steam vegetables lightly; don't cook away all the nutrients.

- Drink eight to ten 8 oz. glasses of water a day.
- Choose whole grains over processed grains (for example, whole wheat over white bread).
- Watch your protein portion size. The recommended 3 oz. of meat is only about the size of a deck of cards.
- Switch from whole milk to skim or low fat 1%, and choose low-fat cheese over regular.
- Eat fruit instead of goodies.
- Eat three meals a day, plus three small, healthy snacks in between meals.
- Don't eat after 9 PM.

Open large bags of food and portion them into Baggies. That way, you can grab them on the go and you're not tempted to eat more then you should. This works well with chips and cookies. Also try it with vegetables after you cut them up.

A survey by Day-Timers Inc. found that, at least once a week, 53% of working Americans eat at a fast-food restaurant. Forty percent bring home take-out meals. Twenty-three percent cook the main course of a meal in the microwave. And eighteen percent eat frozen prepared meals.

When sautéing use chicken broth instead of oil. It will save you approximately 119 calories and 14 grams of fat!

Non-Traditional Ways to Exercise

You don't always have to just walk on a treadmill or take an aerobics class. Here are some alternatives that will get you moving:

- ➤ Bicycle
- ➤ Dance
- ➤ Swim
- ➤ Clean
- ➤ Hike
- ➤ Park far away and walk.
- ➤ Play with your kids.
- ➤ Walk with a friend or your spouse.
- ➤ Get off the bus a stop earlier and walk.
- ➤ Take the stairs, not the elevator, at least for one floor.

Make family members', yearly check-ups with the doctor around their birthday. That way, you won't forget.

Thirty-six percent of the workforce said they exercise once or twice a month or less. Only 37% said they exercise regularly.

Forty percent of working people skip breakfast. Thirty-nine percent skip lunch. Of those who take a lunch break; 50% allow only 15 minutes or less.

A survey by Day-Timers Inc. found that just 38% of Americans feel they are in good health.

10 Ways to Boost Your Energy

1. Take B vitamins or eat B vitamin-rich foods like avocado, barley, lentils and salmon.
2. Use aromatherapy scents like peppermint, orange or lemon.

3. Get up and move your body. Walk around, stand and stretch, practice yoga or otherwise exercise.
4. Drink peppermint tea or chew mint-flavored gum.
5. View vibrant colors like red and orange.
6. Eat well keeping your blood sugar stable.
7. Eat energy-boosting, nutrient-rich foods like those containing fiber and rich whole foods, not processed foods.
8. Take Ginseng in capsule or liquid form.
9. Sleep right, getting seven to nine hours in every night.
10. Get out into the sun; let your body absorb 10 minutes of sunlight a day.

Most people get six and a half hours or less of sleep a night

Keep a Good Attitude

Attitude is a little thing that makes a big difference. By changing your attitude about something, you can change the entire outcome. Pay attention to how you think about things -- how you talk and how you react. If you notice yourself taking the "glass is half empty" approach to things, try changing your perspective. By looking at things from the positive side life will start to go your way. Your days will seem easier and you'll be happier.

Change your terminology. Instead of saying you have a problem, use the word challenge. And instead of saying you made a mistake, say you learned a lesson.

Make the Most Out of Each Day

A bank credits your account each morning with $86,400. It carries over no balance to tomorrow. Every evening, you

lose the balance you failed to use during the day. What would you do? Draw out every cent, of course!

Each of us has such a back. Its name is time. Every morning, it credits you with 86,400 seconds. Every night, it writes off what you have failed to invest. If you fail to use the day's deposits, the loss is yours. There's no going back.

Invest your time wisely. Get from it the utmost in health, happiness and success! The clock is running. Make the most of your life today.

Some Great Quotes on Attitude

"Our life is what are thoughts make it. Do the best you can, where you are, with what you have."

"Your attitude, almost always determines your altitude in life."

"Life is 10% what happens and 90% how you react to it."

"If you think you can, you're right. If you think you can't, you're right."

"Our lives are not determined by what happens to us, but by how we react to what happens; not by what life brings us, but by the attitude we bring to life. A positive attitude causes a chain reaction of positive thoughts, events, and outcomes. It is a catalyst... a spark that creates extraordinary results."

"Smile, it makes people wonder what you are up to."

 Look for the silver lining there is always one.

Angry people are twice as likely to suffer a heart attack as a person in better control of their emotions.

"The only disability in life is a bad attitude." Scott Hamilton

Watch Your Relationships

The typical American worker in a relationship spends only an average of ten hours a week alone with their partner.

Surrounding yourself with nurturing people is another part of caring for yourself. Spend time with people whose company you enjoy and who make you feel good. Those are the relationships that you should spend time on strengthening.

Steer away from high maintenance, draining relationships. It's easy to spot this type of person. In a relationship you're always giving, and you feel exhausted after spending time together. You don't look forward to your time with this person. These people can be close friends, family members or co-workers.

No amount of organizing or managing will make you feel good without connecting to others. I can tell you right now that you won't get it all done alone. So take time for family, friends and yourself.

Nurturing your relationships is an important aspect of taking care of yourself. Having someone who you know will stick with you through it all is very important, whether it's a spouse, life partner, best friend or close family member. Taking care of those relationship takes effort.

See how many of the following statements are true for you; consider working on the ones that are not.

- ➢ I've told my parents that I love them in the last three months.
- ➢ I get along with my siblings.
- ➢ I get along with my co-workers.
- ➢ I get along with my manager/boss.
- ➢ There's no one I would mind running into on the street.
- ➢ I have closure on all my past relationships.
- ➢ I have let go of bad relationships and/or corrected bad ways people treat me.
- ➢ I have friends and other nourishing relationships.
- ➢ I have apologized to those I have wronged.
- ➢ I am caught up on my correspondences; I have no outstanding calls to make or letters to write.
- ➢ I set boundaries and don't get taken advantage of.
- ➢ I tell people what I want and need.
- ➢ I always tell the truth.
- ➢ I have forgiven people who have hurt me.
- ➢ I correct miscommunications as soon as they occur.
- ➢ I don't take things personally.
- ➢ I spend time with people I enjoy being around and who make me feel good.

Want to be around people with the same interests as you? Start a group. Most public libraries and large chain bookstores will let you meet there for free. For example, you could start a reading or writing group.

The average working person, who is married, spends less than two minutes a day in meaningful communication with their spouse and less than 30 minutes per day in meaningful communication with their children.

Turn off the television during a conversation.

Spend more time with your kids by having bedtime talks, walking them to and/or home from school, playing a game after dinner, watching a weekly television show together, taking your children out for dinner to a restaurant of their choice, or building a puzzle.

Pay bills at the table while kids do homework it is not what you are doing while you are together it's just that you are together

In this day and age of technology it can be a big deal when there is a blackout. This is the story of a client who turned a blackout into a memorable experience. It was a hot and humid summer night, things were going along as usual. Her husband was on the Internet, her son was playing video games and her daughter was talking on the phone. Each family member was caught up in their own world doing their own thing. When all of a sudden the lights flickered a few times and then went out. The air conditioner ground to a halt, the television died, the computer screen went black and the cordless phone disconnected. Suddenly three grumpy family members surrounded her. They demanded to know when the power would be back on. After a few minutes of dealing with her family, she suggested something novel; why not spend some time together? At first they were a little confused by this concept, it had been so long since it had last happened. Slowly they warmed up to the idea. They lit candles and sat around and talked, they told each other what had been going on in all their lives. They were so engrossed telling stories and laughing that they didn't even realize when the lights came back on. Since that night the family has had a "blackout party" once a month. They turn off everything in the house, phone, television, computer, radio, everything. And they do something together. Talking, playing cards, and looking at photos are some of the most popular activities. During the winter, when they have a fire roaring in the fireplace, they even toast marshmallows.

 Have a backwards day. Eat dessert before dinner. Sit in chairs backwards. Wear your clothes backwards.

Stagger bedtimes so you can read/talk to each child individually.

Never underestimate the power of a nap!

Ninety-five percent of divorces are caused by a "lack of communication."

"The only way to have a friend is to be one." Ralph Waldo Emerson

Practice Random Acts of Kindness

Touch someone's heart in some way each and every day.
Here are some ideas:

- ➤ Let a car go in front of you.
- ➤ Drop goodies off at a local fire station or hospital.
- ➤ Bring fresh flowers to a nursing home.
- ➤ Pay the toll for the car behind you.
- ➤ Pay for the movie tickets for the couple behind you.
- ➤ Give another driver your parking space.
- ➤ Let the person behind you in line at the store go ahead of you.
- ➤ Brush snow off a stranger's car in a parking lot.
- ➤ Rake your next-door neighbor's leaves.

Nurture the Relationship with Your Spouse

Here's thirty ways to show your spouse that you care. Try these ideas out. What else can you think of?

1. Call your spouse just to say, "I love you."
2. Compliment your spouse at least once a day.
3. Let the answering machine pickup your calls so you can concentrate on each other.
4. Eat dinner by candlelight.
5. Talk about a favorite memory you have of the two of you together.
6. Bring morning coffee or juice to your spouse while they're still in bed.
7. Really look at each other when you're talking.
8. Massage your spouse's feet.
9. Hold hands while you're watching television.
10. Eat a bowl of ice cream together after the kids go to bed.
11. Turn off the television and do something together.

12. While your spouse is in the shower, toss a towel in the dryer and bring it to him/her when he/she gets out of the shower.
13. Make a pact with yourself to not get upset over the next thing your spouse does that annoys you.
14. Use sidewalk chalk to write your names in a heart on the driveway.
15. Put on your spouse's favorite music.
16. Write a letter and tell your spouse why you would marry them all over again.
17. Place a little note in your spouse's lunch or briefcase.
18. Instead of just giving your spouse a peck hello or goodbye, give them a deep kiss and hold onto them for a few seconds.
19. Bring him/her flowers for no reason.
20. If your spouse is usually the one to pay for the gas, then next time you stop you pay.
21. Give your spouse the best piece of chicken at dinner or the newspaper section he/she likes first even -- if you want to read it.
22. Play footsie at the table.
23. When your spouse is telling a story, ask a question about it.
24. Put your wedding song on tape or CD and place it in his/her car stereo.
25. Send an e-mail or fax or leave a voice mail message saying you cannot wait to see him/her later that day.
26. Make your spouse his/her favorite meal and top it off with a sinful dessert.
27. The next time you're with family or friends, tell them about something great your spouse just did that you're proud of.
28. Get out your wedding pictures and look at them or watch your wedding video
29. Get up with the baby when it's not your turn and let your spouse sleep
30. Send your spouse a card with a love note.

Studies show that the first three minutes you spend with your spouse at the end of the day set the tone for the entire evening.

Dear Abby helps us with a list of "Ten Rules for a Happy Marriage." This list was sent to her from a couple who reached their 50th anniversary and successfully made their marriage a promise for life.

Rule #1	Never both be angry at the same time.
Rule #2	Never yell at each other unless the house is on fire.
Rule #3	If one of you has to win an argument let it be your mate.
Rule #4	If you must criticize, do it lovingly.
Rule #5	Never bring up mistakes of the past.
Rule #6	Neglect the whole world rather than each other.
Rule #7	Never go to sleep with an argument unsettled.
Rule #8	At least once a day, say a kind or complimentary word to your mate.
Rule #9	When you have done something wrong, admit it and ask forgiveness.
Rule #10	Remember that it takes two to make a quarrel.

"To keep love brimming... when you're wrong admit it and when you're right shut up." Odgen Nash

"You cannot do a kindness too soon, for you never know how soon it will be too late." Ralph Waldo Emerson

Feel Better About Yourself

"No one can make you feel inferior without your consent." Eleanor Roosevelt

Our own self-esteem is not something we think about often. But having low esteem can be a cause for a variety of issues in your life. We all suffer from low esteem at some point. Inevitability there will be times when we're not as good at something as others. Those of us who have high self-esteem will rebound quickly. But for those who could use higher esteem, here are some great ways to get a big boost:

> ➢ Make a list of five to ten things you have done in the last few months that make you proud of yourself.
> ➢ Surround yourself with people who like and appreciate you just the way you are.
> ➢ Become aware of the negative thoughts you have and immediately replace them with a positive statement.
> ➢ Start to be okay with messing up, everyone does.
> ➢ Practice good posture; it will boost your spirits!
> ➢ Stop comparing yourself to someone you think is better, prettier, smarter, or thinner.
> ➢ Accept your emotions. It's okay to feel sad or angry.
> ➢ Practice sitting up straight and looking people in the eyes when you talk to them.
> ➢ Stop putting your life on hold until you lose weight, have more money, time and so on. Do one thing right now that you have been putting off until things are "better."
> ➢ Do something for the outside of your body, and you'll get a boost on the inside. Buy a new outfit,

113

get a new haircut, or have your makeup professionally applied.

➤ Speak up; your ideas are as good and important as anyone else's. Remember all those times that someone said just what you were thinking.

These are all excellent ideas. Try out a few and watch your self-esteem rise. When you feel better about yourself, you automatically feel better about life.

I recently worked with a client who was looking to meet someone she could be in a relationship with. She found her mate on the night when she went out to dinner with a friend in a brand new outfit and an updated hairstyle. Meeting her mate is not attributed to the fact that she looked good, although she did. But she *felt* good. The new outfit and hairstyle on the outside gave her a new found confidence that radiated from her.

"Love yourself first and everything else falls into line. You really have to love yourself to get anything done in this world." Lucille Ball

Face your fears; facing them increases your confidence.

Stop second-guessing yourself if it's not a life or death decision choose and adjust later if you must.

Forget past failures. Learn from them and try again. The past is just that, in the past

It's important to talk to others if you feel you're the only one with a particular problem. Guaranteed, others have dealt with it and they may have helpful advice or at least can sympathize.

Are you longing for a little more of something in your life? More understanding? More love? More appreciation? Use "the give to get theory." Give out what you want more of. For example, if you're wishing you would get more appreciation, then try making a concerted effort to truly appreciate others. Thank them, tell them what a great job they are doing, and you'll be amazed how soon others will be showing their appreciation of your efforts.

Remember your worth is not based on how clean your house is or how thin you are.

Lifting your Confidence
Remind yourself that even the most confident people get frazzled from time to time you are not alone. But feeling less than confident all the time can cause you to be unhappy. So lift your confidence level by training yourself to feel good. Think of one or two things that make you feel happy -- a special place, a memory, music or a joke. Whenever you need a boost, just remember and you will instantly feel good. And keep in mind that people can rarely tell when you feel less than confident about yourself. Act confident and you will come across as confident. It's the old "fake it until you make it" routine.

Feeling self-conscious? One way to combat it is to take the spotlight off yourself. Instead of standing around feeling anxious, do something. Involve yourself in a conversation, help out in the kitchen, or go up to someone who is by him-or-herself and introduce yourself.

Also become aware of how you talk to yourself. Stop self-criticism and just be you. Don't try to be like others, accept yourself. Repeating affirmations will give your self-confidence a boost. Here are some suggestions:

> I deserve to be happy and successful.
> I make my own choices.
> I am satisfied with doing my best.
> I have the power to change myself.

Write your favorite affirmation on an index card. Keep it handy where you'll see it. Say it often.

Ninety-five percent of the things we fear, do not occur.

A recent survey found that 75% of women and 54% of men reported that they are unhappy with their physical appearance.

Feel Better About Your Body
Many people -- not just women suffer from a negative body image. And how can we help it with all the ads and commercials showing thin, pretty people having a great time in life? Well, remember that they are just models, that's not real life. Here are some ways to improve your body image.

First, it's helpful to have a self-improvement partner. It can be a family member, co-worker, friend, spouse or any other person who you trust. They should have the same goals as you -- whatever that means to you. And start off by creating your own definition of "beautiful." Beauty is not only on the outside, and it's certainly not just 5'10" and 110 pounds. Set your own guidelines and standards without worrying about who is gracing the cover of the magazines this month.

In addition, stop concerning yourself with the numbers on the scale. In fact consider tossing away your scale altogether. I often hear statements like "Oh my life will be so much better once I lose X number of pounds." Think about it, what would really be different? The only thing different about your life then would be your weight - nothing else will have changed. Stop talking about weight. You will probably be surprised how preoccupied we are with weight. Start paying attention to how many times you and the people around you make reference to weight during the course of one day.

Stop worrying about what others think about you. Changing your self-image may not be about changing yourself but rather about accepting yourself. Think about it!

Your Environment
Your environment consists of so many things. Who and what is around you makes a huge difference in the quality of your life. By surrounding yourself with stressful people, clutter and demanding tasks you undoubtedly will have a stressful life. So then by the same reasoning if your life is full of supportive people, you are organized and tasks are easy your life will be peaceful. So set yourself up for good and comfy living by:

> ➢ Surrounding yourself with nice stuff.
> ➢ Finding beautiful and meaningful things to keep around.
> ➢ Using uplifting colors to decorate with.
> ➢ Spending time with nurturing people.

➤ Limiting your access to disturbing nightly news reports, violent movies, suspenseful television shows.
➤ Keeping fresh flowers around.

Remember that smells are a very big part of your environment. Just think of how good you feel when you smell cookies baking or coffee brewing. Consider enhancing your surrounding by using:

➤ Scented candles
➤ Lamp rings with scented oils
➤ Incense
➤ Carpet powders
➤ Air fresheners

Which one sounds most like you? Challenge yourself....

Eager Pleaser
When your husband asks you where you want to go for dinner, you answer, "Where ever you like." This is even though you are in the mood for Chinese.

Challenge yourself: Say "no" to at least one person a day when you would have normally agreed to it. And the next time someone asks you something actually tell him or her your opinion. When your husband asks what you'd like for dinner and you say Chinese, you just might get it. You'll be surprised by how much others respect your wishes once you tell them what you want.

Worrywart
You have trouble falling asleep at night because you're trying to figure out how you'll do everything you need to do tomorrow.

Challenge yourself: Stop playing "what if" and "I should have" games with yourself takes you out of the present. Learn to live in the moment. Enjoy the fact that you're alive and well. Trust that what needs to get done will get done.

Stop finishing this sentence, "What if...?" You have a great imagination and you're able to come up with outrageous things to worry about. These things very rarely come true. Work on not allowing yourself to become overwhelmed by the "what ifs" you create.

Miss Perfect
Your daughter folded the towels in quarters instead of in thirds like you taught her, so you redo them.

Challenge yourself: Give yourself a well-deserved break and stop holding yourself up to impossible standards. Do the best you can and be satisfied with that.

Control Queen
Your son needs help on a school project. You start off by simply lending a hand. Before you know it, you have changed everything and discover that your son has retreated to his room.

Challenge yourself: Stop expending time and energy trying to have everyone live up to your expectations. Practice letting go and you'll start to notice their unique gifts and learn to treasure them.

Adrenaline Junkie
You need a cup of coffee to get yourself going every morning, and you eat sweets throughout the day to give yourself a boost.

Challenge yourself: Living fast can cause you to lose touch, and it can be dangerous to your health. Practice doing one task at a time and do it slowly. Consider weaning yourself off the caffeine by pouring only a half a cup of regular coffee and half a cup of decaf.

Identifying and meeting *your* needs. That's what it's all about. It may be difficult at first. However once you set aside time for you, you'll begin to look forward to your time outs.

Chapter Highlights:
- Schedule free time during which you can take care of yourself.
- Journal at least three times a week.
- Eat healthy, drink plenty of water, exercise and get enough sleep.
- Identify and eliminate "tolerations."
- Give up control.
- Ask for what you want.
- Teach people to treat you how you want to be treated.

Chapter Resources
- *Journaling* magazine
- Journaling site
- Ms. Basia Conroy
  Re-Vitalizations
  66 Point View Parkway
  Wayne, NJ 07470
  973-628-8718
  Practicalspiritual@earthlink.com
  She is a Life Coach, Corporate Trainer, Author and Speaker who facilitates workshops on the "Heart of Creativity" and more.
- Journey-The Metaphysical Boutique
  Woodbrige Center Mall
  US Hwy. Route 1
  Woodbridge, NJ 07095
  (732) 636-8141

- www. scentsnsensibility.com
- www.journalingmagazine.com
- www.journalforyou.com
- www.comfortqueen.com
- www.journalsunlimited.com
- Cranford Herbs and Acupuncture
  Gerard Reidy, Jr. CA
  908-612-5698
  1 Walnut Ave, Cranford, NJ 07016
  GerardCReidyJr@hotmail.com
- Success Express
  http://www.ataclick.com/ataclick/cgi-bin/member.cgi?MerchantID=561&Group=2
- www.flip10-dramatix.com
- www.campsark.com
- www.runningrhino.com
- American Massage Therapy Association
  www.amtamassage.org - 847-864-0123
- www.spafinders.com
- www.newage.com – *Body and Soul Magazine*
- www.realsimple.com - *Real Simple* magazine
- Petfinder.org - An incredible website where you can find adoption information on just about any animal you are looking for. You can search by type of animal, age, size, sex and more. Also there are pictures, detailed descriptions and lots of other helpful information.
- Life U Love – 1-866-294-9900
  369 Evergreen Blvd.
  Scotch Plains, NJ 07076
  www.lifeulove.com – jamie@lifeulove.com

Next find that something which is missing in your life.
AKA Finding Your Passion and Spirit

This section is for you if any of the following apply:

- ➤ I long for something more or different.
- ➤ I feel something is missing from my life.
- ➤ I often feel sad or angry.
- ➤ I regret many choices that I have made in my life.
- ➤ I feel like something is wrong with how I am living.
- ➤ I don't have anything to look forward to these days.

"Life isn't about finding yourself. Life is about creating yourself." George Bernard Shaw

> ### The Essence of Destiny
>
> Watch your thoughts,
> For they become words.
> Choose your words,
> For they become actions.
> Understand your actions,
> For they become habits.
> Study your habits,
> For they become your
> character.
> Develop your character,
> For it becomes your destiny.
> Author Unknown

Introduction

You don't need to create passion or spirit; they have been there all along. You may need to coax them or listen closely. Your passion and spirit are like muscles; they communicate through your feelings and intuition. The more you use them, the stronger they get and the stronger the feelings will become. So trust your gut.

Do what you think you can't or what you fear the most. Breaking through fear is half the battle.

Fire your guru. Take action by getting books and tapes that then inspire you to do something.

You won't regret trying and failing, you'll regret never trying.

123

Shake it up! Rearrange a room or drive home a different route from work. Break up the monotony.

Getting in touch with passion and spirit will help you find your place in life. You'll feel more a part of the world around you. So know that you're where you belong and trust that what's happening is supposed to be happening. Everything occurs for a reason.

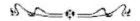

What's Your Passion?
For many people the image that comes to mind when they hear the word "passion" is like the cover of a romance novel. There's a stunningly beautiful gal in the arms of a hunky male hero. While that picture does portray passion of the romantic kind, I'm talking about a passion for *life*. It's a feeling of contentment, being secure in the knowledge that you've made the right choices. You're happy *right now* with the current state of your life and the direction you've chosen.

Some people have a passion for their jobs that satisfies them. Others volunteer and give of themselves to fulfill their sense of passion. But still other folk have yet to find something that really gets them going -- something they're proud about and look forward to doing. I often hear people who are still searching for their passion say things like "If I just had…" or "As soon as I…" or "When I…." These are all examples of waiting for passion to come to you instead of *seeking out your passion*. I also hear people complain that they don't know their life's purpose or they're wondering what they're supposed to be doing. If you find yourself waiting and questioning, then grab a pen and paper and answer the following:

1. If there was no way that you could fail, what would you do?
2. If money were not a concern in your life, what would you be doing right now?
3. When you daydream, what do you daydream about doing?
4. What adjectives describe you?
5. How would you like to be remembered after your death?
6. What did you always love doing as a child?
7. What subjects do you enjoy reading about?
8. What are people always telling you that you're good at?
9. What are your greatest talents?
10. What were your favorite subjects in school?
11. What television shows do you enjoy watching?
12. What do you love to do?
13. If you could have any kind of job, what would it be?
14. What are your favorite kinds of people?
15. What are your hobbies?
16. What were your favorite toys?
17. What type of volunteer work do you do?
18. What would you do right now if you weren't afraid what others might think or say?
19. What subjects do you enjoy discussing with friends?
20. In years gone by, what was important to you?
21. When you look at the clock and cannot believe how much time has passed what was it that had you so captivated?

Now take a look at your answers. What threads of similarity do you see running through them? Are your bookshelves packed with recipe books? Do people always compliment you on your cooking? Do you enjoy experimenting with recipes? Are you forever critiquing your meals when you're out to eat? You don't necessarily need to quit your job to become a chef but you might consider taking a cooking class or even teaching one at the local adult school. Imagine the fun that you would have meeting new people that have interests similar to yours. That would be something to be passionate about!

Be careful not to confuse skill with talent. Don't look just at what you can do. Just because you can do it doesn't mean you like to do it. You may be a great typist; on your current job, you may have learned to type 80 words a minute. That doesn't mean your dream job is as a typist.

Go back to your pen and paper and complete the following:

> I can do the following well...
> I am mainly interested in...
> I believe most in...
>   I most value...
> To live a life I love, I need...

Start small. If you think you might like to be a teacher, then try teaching a local adult class on a subject you're good at or volunteer to be a teacher's aide.

Eighty percent of people do not want to go to work Monday morning. Ninety-seven percent say that if they won the lottery or achieved financial independence, they would not go back to work at all or go back to doing what they're doing now.

Turn your current job into your dream job. If you dream of having a different job, see if you can take on some job responsibilities that you like and delegate those that you're not crazy about.

Once you identify something that sounds like a lot of fun, you need to take steps towards bringing it into your life. For example, if you enjoy cooking, then look for places that offer cooking classes. Sign up or explore how you might be able to teach a class. Whatever it is for you, take some step -- no matter how small or big, towards your goal. It's the only way to recapture or create passion in your life. Once you have something to fill the void you'll feel more satisfied with your life.

Forty-nine percent of workers in America complain that they're on a treadmill.

Don't talk yourself out of trying something new. The only way to know for sure if what you wish for will make you happy is to go for it!

Seventy-eight percent of workers in America wish they had more time to smell the roses.

But what if you don't have any dreams? Do you feel that you have no passions? No sense of any gifts, talents, purpose or calling? Be silent and it will come.

A few years ago I met a woman at one of my lectures that claimed she had no passion in her life. After the lecture we spoke at length about what she meant. She explained that her days were all the same. She woke up and went to work as a bookkeeper, and then she came home and watched television or read a book until it was time for her to go to bed. Then she woke up in the morning and did it all over again. She admitted she was having a hard time waking up in the morning and no matter how early she went to bed she was still tired. I asked her a series of questions that got her thinking about what she enjoyed doing. I wanted to know what some of her hobbies had been and what types of books she enjoyed reading. Once she thought about some of the things I was asking her she realized that she did enjoy reading, she loved walking through bookstores just browsing around. So we brainstormed about ways that she could get involved with books. Some thoughts were selling books on Ebay, a part-time job in a bookstore, and volunteering in a library. She decided to take this list of ideas and add to it. We spoke a week later and she had a plan, she had taken a part-time job working two evenings and Saturdays at a local used bookstore. She was going to be in charge of the community programs like reading to children and hosting weekly book clubs. She was very excited about the position and had already started planning events. Not only would she be around books and people who enjoyed reading, but she would be making a little extra money as well. She called me a few months later to update me on how the job was going. She loved the work. She had met some really nice people, she has even become good friends with a few ladies and they did group things like go to watch plays. She now looked forward to waking each day and had a sense of satisfaction at the end of every day.

What about spirit?
If you spend most of your time being who you're expected to be -- for your family, friends, bosses and others -- somewhere in all that, you can get lost. You may not know who you are anymore, and when you're lying in bed at night ready to fall asleep and the world is quiet, that may scare you. Start by paying attention to your actions and your words. When do you feel good? Happy? Full of energy? At the best times, who are you with and what are

you doing? Start being true to your newly found self and stop doing what you always did.

"*Relax. Live your life and keep your eyes on your dreams. Le the rest work itself out along the way.*" Author Unknown

Nurture Your Spirit
Here are a dozen ways to foster your spirit.

1. Create a quiet space.
2. Sit in silence or soft sounds.
3. Surround yourself with wonderful scents.
4. Practice random acts of kindness.
5. Reassess your beliefs.
6. Stop trying to control life.
7. Live in the moment.
8. Learn your lessons.
9. Cause and effect -- Do to others as you would have them do to you.
10. Watch your motives; why are you doing something?
11. Celebrate Nature.
12. Give up scarcity thinking; there will always be enough.

Once you find out what will make you happy, it's your responsibility to start finding ways to make it happen. No matter what it is, taking even small steps toward your goal will make your life exciting. You'll look forward to each new day with energy and enthusiasm.

Chapter Highlights
- Stop putting your life on hold.
- Discover what you get passionate about.
- Take action towards fulfilling your passion deficit.

- Make time for nurturing your spirit.

Chapter Resources
- *Wishcraft* by Barbara Sheer
- Life U Love – 1-866-294-9900
  369 Evergreen Blvd.
  Scotch Plains, NJ 07076
  www.lifeulove.com – jamie@lifeulove.com

Now find out how much money you make and where it all goes.
AKA Getting a Handle on Your Finances

This section is for you if any of the following apply:

- ➤ I save less than 10% of my income.
- ➤ I save little or nothing toward retirement.
- ➤ My money gets little or no return.
- ➤ I am late paying some or most of my bills.
- ➤ I am not sure if I need life insurance.
- ➤ I owe back taxes.
- ➤ I am not sure if my salary is equal to the effort I put out at work.

Getting Started

There are some basic ideas regarding finances that work well for everyone. I'm not a financial planner but I do know that making more money than you spend is a good idea. In order to do that, you need to know how much you make and where the money goes. Do you ever look at the year-to-date amount on your paycheck stub and wonder where you spent all that money? If so, then now is a good time to start by tracking your expenses. How much do you spend on taxes, debt, food and rent/mortgage? Creating a

131

budget you'll stick to is a very good idea. That way you're sure to cover your expenses and still have money to save. You also need to balance your checkbook monthly; you'll want to know how much money you have right now.

Don't Forget Savings

Saving money is a key idea in finance. Even if you can only stash away $25 a month, it's something and the money will grow. The trick is to consistently put the money aside before you are tempted to spend it. I've heard many financial planners say, "Pay yourself first." One way to ensure that you do is to have some money automatically withdrawn from your checking account on a monthly basis and transferred into some sort of a savings account. Many financial institutions offer Electronic Funds Transfers or EFTs that allow you to transfer as little as $25 a month. Still, having your money sitting somewhere that earns you a high rate of return will give you more incentive to save. Consider money markets or mutual funds instead of the more traditional methods like savings accounts and Certificates of Deposit (CDs). Wouldn't it give you peace of mind to know that you have a few months' salary stashed in the event of an emergency?

 Save 10% of any bonuses you receive.

 When you get a raise, deposit it into savings. You lived without it before the raise.

 Work overtime to reach a goal. Example: A new outfit costing $55. Save for it, don't charge it on your credit card and then figure out how to pay for it when the bill comes in.

$5 a day on a café latte equals $150 a month. This equates to $1,800 a year -- on coffee! Consider buying regular coffee every day and treat yourself occasionally.

Costs due to chaos, late fees and paying last minute can eat up over 20% of your budget.

Next Step - Your Bills and Credit Cards
Now that you've thought about savings, let's look at another important area of finance - bills and credit cards. First, you might make bill-paying easier by choosing to pay most of your bills one time a month. Take a look at the due dates on your bills. Are they all around the same time or spread out throughout the month? You can call your creditors and request that they change your due date. Most creditors will, though not all. When the majority of your due dates are around the same time, you can simply pay all of these bills at once. Many creditors are now offering the option to have your bills paid automatically - often in return for a reduction in your interest rate. Consider this option or look at banking online -- no more checks to write or trips to the post office to buy stamps!

Keep an envelope just for credit card receipts. Then when the bill comes in, you can staple the envelope to the statement. This makes receipts easy to find. You can also make sure the statement is correct and you'll have the receipts for returns or exchanges.

Order your credit report once a year from the top three reporting agencies -- Equifax, Experian and Transunion -- check it over for errors. Don't overlook ordering your Social Security statement. It's a valuable document that estimates your future Social Security benefits. You can call the Social Security Administration toll-free and request a statement of your benefits. The number is 1-800-772-1213. Or visit their website to request the statement online or to download a form to mail in. Their website is www.ssa.gov.

Million Dollar Retirement

Goal: A cool million at age 65 to retire with. Earning 10% on your money, here is what you'd have to put away annually.

If You Start at Age	Amount You Need to Invest Per Year
20	1,391
30	3,690
40	10,168
Over	31,474

How many credit cards do you have? Try to simplify by transferring all your outstanding credit card balances to the card with the lowest interest rate. Then close the other accounts and keep just the one account active and up-to-date. If you have other outstanding debts, you need to know what they are and have a plan to pay them off. Even if the plan is to pay the minimum plus a little every month, you know you're working towards paying them off.

The snowball effect is a great way to get out of debt. It works like this; list all your bills with their interest rates next to them. Find the one with the highest interest rate; maybe it is a Visa card. Now pay the monthly minimum on all your bills and pay whatever extra you can to the Visa bill. You will be on your way towards paying off Visa. Once you do, take the money that you were sending to Visa and apply it to the next debt on your list. Once that bill is paid off entirely, take that money and apply it to the next card on the list. Before you know it, you're paying triple or more than the minimum payment and fast on your way out of debt!

If you're unable to pay a bill, call before the due date and make arrangements. Most companies are happy to make payment arrangements. For example: A client had a major emergency car repair that required her to take out a loan with a local bank. In December she looked at her budget. She realized she would not have enough money to buy Christmas gifts and make the loan payment. She immediately called the bank and explained the situation. The bank noted her account and allowed her to pay half her normal payment. She avoided the stress of falling behind or receiving collection calls, while saving her credit rating and maintaining a working relationship with the bank. The customer service representative even thanked her for calling ahead of time and wished her a happy holiday.

Adding a $25 a week payment for something may not seem like a lot but four of these make an extra $100 a month! That can make a big difference in a budget.

Fee-based checking accounts, ATM charges, and bounced checked fees are all unnecessary expenses to watch out for.

Comparison shop with *Consumer Reports* but go to the library instead of subscribing. Use your energy wisely; shop around for things like a mortgage -- not a toaster.

Watch out for debt traps. If you have an installment loan, you'll receive offers that allow you to defer payments, to write checks by adding the amount to your loan, or to accept more pre-approved money. Try not to take advantage of these tempting offers. Remember, you want to get out of debt while the loan company would be perfectly happy if you stay in debt.

Have you ever been dissatisfied enough with a product or service to call or write the company? How about *satisfied* enough? Many companies have discounts and coupons reserved for their loyal customers. All you have to do is ask. I have a few clients who routinely call companies whose products and/or services they use. They express how pleased they are and in return the companies offer coupons or a 10% plus reduction in their bill that month. It takes a few minutes to make a call or write a letter, but it is well worth the effort.

No More Payday Bank Lines!
Remember that you want to keep dealing with your finances as simple as possible. One great way to do this is to have your paycheck directly deposited into your checking and/or savings account every payday. You can choose what percentage of your check you want deposited into which account; what could be simpler? No more running to the bank on payday and wasting time sitting in line.

 Let's say you have $10,000 on a credit card charging 19% interest. If you only paid the minimum payments, this would take you 30 years to pay off!

Close all unused accounts.

Those Matters you've Been Delaying
As with all areas of life, there can be financial matters that you have been meaning to take care of but just have not gotten around to yet. I often hear people say they have to update their will and living will. And lots of times, there

136

are 401Ks that should be rolled over which you have not gotten to yet. Do you need to update the beneficiary designation on your mutual funds or insurance? Are you, your family and your assets protected with enough and the right types of insurances? Do you have lingering investments that need to be wrapped up? If so, make an appointment to have this handled. If you're unsure about who to speak to regarding such important issues, consider talking to a trusted friend to see who they deal with.

Break down what you make into hourly wages. That way you can see the cost of things. For example, a haircut may be $30. If you make $10 an hour; that's three hours of work.

Ponder Purchases
Keep in mind when dealing with your finances that it's better to buy time and not things. The more things you have, the more time you need to spend caring for them. This means there's less time for you and the more important things. Skip the unnecessary purchases. A good way to do this is every time you want to buy something, write it down on a list. Wait to buy it for at least fifteen days. If after fifteen days you still want this, then go ahead and buy it. If it's a purchase that you don't really have the money for, then take a look at how you can save the money. For example: if you want to go away for a weekend, have a housekeeper come in once that month rather than weekly. Or look for something else you can cut out -- like buying your lunch. Bring it from home instead.

Keep your checkbook on Quicken, QuickBooks, Microsoft Money or some other software program. This prevents math errors and makes reconciling easy.

In One Hand, Out the Other?

Another great area to take a look at is where you are throwing money away. Do you pay for any memberships that aren't used enough to make them worthwhile? How about subscriptions that you may have to magazines and newspapers? Are there any that you may not have time to read or read just out of habit and not pleasure? Is there an outfit you bought that you have not worn yet because it's just not right? Can you return it? Have you received CDs or books from an automatic membership but don't want them? Do you belong to a gym or a pool with high membership fees? Lastly, take a look at why you buy some things. Do you buy them because you truly want or need them or because you're trying to keep up with the Joneses? By making purchases for the right reasons and keeping your finances in check, you'll be making huge strides towards living a life you love!

Watch out for the easy-to-fall-for upgrades. When buying an item, deliberate about the extras you can get for a few dollars more. Do you really need a television set that gives you picture in picture or the cell phone with games and screen savers? To some people, these are important and they make a conscious decision to spend the extra money. But, in most cases, we're easily persuaded to get the top of the line when we really don't need it. Also read the paperwork, are you being signed up for a maintenance plan on an item that you do not want or need? If so do not accept it.

Security does not come from having a pile of money stashed somewhere. True security is having reserves in many areas; finances are only one of them. Other important areas include community, family and friends, faith, confidence, health, love and self-esteem.

Don't Forget Your Children
Teach kids how to handle money with an allowance. In this way, children can learn how to budget too. They'll and realize that once the money is gone, it's gone. Help them start a savings or investment plan so they can watch their money grow.

 Give children extra money for non-routine jobs like helping box up items for a garage sale.

 Some suggestions of free things to do as a family:

➢ Go on a picnic	➢ Take a walk in the forest or on a nature trail
➢ Borrow a canoe and ride down a river	➢ Go sled riding
➢ Go for a drive and look at the fall leaves	➢ Camp out in your backyard
➢ Watch a fireworks display	➢ Go fishing
➢ Watch the stars and/or a meteor shower	➢ Make popcorn and watch a movie (on TV or borrow a video from a friend)

Learning about your finances is the first step. You have to know what you have before you can decide what to do with it. Ignoring your financial situation just causes stress; it does not make it go away. So track your expenses and your earnings and go from there.

Please refer to the Budget Worksheet located in the back of the book.

Chapter Highlights

- Spend less than you make.
- Know how much money you make and where it goes.
- Have a financial plan and stick to it.
- Have a get-out-of-debt plan and stick to it.
- Save money on a regular basis -- no matter how little.
- Make sure you have enough and the right kind of insurance.

- **Chapter Resources**
- Debt Counselors of America – www.dca.org
  800-680-3328
- www.bankrate.com - Objective information on many financial matters
- Consumer Credit Counseling Service - 800-388-2227 non-profit free confidential financial counseling.
- Quicken.com
- QuickBooks
- MS Money
- Institute of certified financial planners – www.icfp.org
  303-759-4900
- American Institute of CPA – www.aicpa.org
- Suzie Orman, Author
- Thomas J. Stanley, *Millionaire Next Door*
- Richard Carson, *Don't Worry, Make Money*
- www.Equifax.com
- www.experian.com
- www.transunion.com
- Consumer Reports
- Life U Love – 1-866-294-9900
  369 Evergreen Blvd.

Scotch Plains, NJ 07076
www.lifeulove.com – jamie@lifeulove.com

Then teach yourself to juggle your work and other life.
AKA Balancing Work and Life

This section is for you if any of the following out-of-balance warning signs apply to you:

- ➢ You cannot attend to childcare emergencies.
- ➢ You rarely see your family.
- ➢ You forget important things.
- ➢ You cannot accommodate family responsibilities that are significant to you.
- ➢ Your spouse resorts to ultimatums to get some of your time.
- ➢ You feel tired when you wake up.
- ➢ You feel as though you cannot face one more day of work.
- ➢ Your life is not working the way you want it to work.
- ➢ You feel as though you're working too hard for too little reward.
- ➢ You're drained by the end of the day.
- ➢ You're often in a bad mood.
- ➢ You have little patience.
- ➢ You resent your job and/or responsibilities.

➤ You cannot remember the last time you enjoyed yourself.

➤ You suffer from a stress-related condition – a rash, migraines, stomachaches, etc.

Introduction

No one ever died wishing they had spent more time at work. So how do you fulfill your responsibilities to your family without getting fired? In this section, we'll discuss techniques for creating a balance between your work life and your life outside work. As you read this section, keep in mind that there is no one way that works for everyone. The trick is going to be to find *your* way.

In the last 20 years, work time has increased by 15% while leisure time has decreased by 33%.

15 Ways to Put Your Life Back in Balance
1. Concentrate on top priorities.
2. Delegate.
3. Avoid time-wasters like meetings.
4. Limit out-of-town travel.
5. Take one afternoon off and see if your co-workers survive without you. (They will.)
6. Take work home with you.
7. Keep an updated list of what you do so someone else can fill in.
8. Ask how important it is.
9. Swap days off with spouse to sit with a sick child or investigate sick childcare facilities in your area.
10. Have a backup plan.
11. Work from home.
12. Try job sharing.
13. Learn some stress management techniques, such as meditation, progressive relaxation, etc.
14. Use your vacation time.
15. Get assistance with eldercare.

To achieve life/work balance, your must realize that money is not everything. You also have to take into account stress, life satisfaction, personal happiness, you connections to family and friends and your health.

See how many of the following statements are true for you. For the ones that aren't true but are important to you, consider making changes.

> - I'm peaceful and happy with my life choices
> - I have time for the things I want to do
> - I don't miss my children's events (games, recitals, meets, etc.).
> - I read for pleasure.
> - I spend enough time with family and friends.
> - I contribute to my community.
> - I exercise.
> - I have a hobby or take a class.
> - I feel in control.
> - I take and enjoy vacation.
> - I take breaks and eat lunch away from my desk.
> - I leave work on time.
> - I get enough sleep and feel rested in the morning.

In this chapter I'm suggesting ways to condense your workday by working smarter, not harder; you probably work too hard already. Many of the ideas focus on time management. By finding more time in your day, you'll be able to arrive at work just a little bit early and leave work on time. Usually this is the first step in gaining work/life balance.

So how do they do it? Your co-workers I mean. The ones who walk into work fifteen minutes early with their homemade lunch in hand. They have time to make a cup of coffee and relax before jumping into their work. These people seem to have no stress, and they glide through their workday eventually wrapping up everything and walking out the door on time. Meanwhile you rush out the door, at home, forget your lunch, drop the kids at school, race to work, and you always seem to get behind the slowest moving car on the face of the earth! Well, your co-workers probably have a system in place. They have created habits that work for them, and they stick with their program. So the question is: What routine can *you* create to make your morning flow smoother?

One good possibility is to prepare for your morning the night before. Pick out your clothes, pack your briefcase, sign all of your children's school papers, and make the lunches (or hand out lunch money). You can even set the table for breakfast, fill the coffeemaker, and load your briefcase into the car.

With no system in place for your mornings, there is chaos. But in contrast, you can create order by having a system that everyone in the family follows. Then once you get to work, you want to settle in before diving into the pile of work on your desk. Chat with co-workers, get yourself something to drink and only then get down to the business of the day.

Working with Your Assistant
If you have an assistant or secretary, you can find ways to work more closely and as a team. And by working as a team, you can get more accomplished with less effort. See what tasks you do yourself under the following categories. Next, see which of these tasks could be delegated to other people on your staff.

Mail/E-mail
Who opens incoming mail and e-mail and responds to routine inquires? Who composes drafts for replies?

Phone Calls
Who answers and screens incoming calls? Who makes sure you follow up on calls?

Filing
Who keeps the files and pulls files that will be needed for the day?

Schedule/Calendar
Who schedules and confirms your appointments?

Follow-Up
Who brings a matter to your attention that requires action?

Meetings
Who reviews agendas prior to meetings? Who takes notes at your meetings or goes as your representative? Who gathers employees for informal meetings? Who types and distributes meeting minutes?

Word Processing
Who composes letters from your key ideas? Who gets you to sign letters and sends them out? Who actually keyboards the letters?

Visitors
Who greets visitors and shows them to your office? Who screens drop-by visitors? Who interrupts if a visitor overstays their welcome?

Time management
Who protects your time from interruption? Who keeps you on track?

Travel
Who makes the travel arrangements? Who creates and distributes your itinerary?

Other

Who ensures equipment is regularly serviced? Who skims articles to determine your interest in reading them?

When instituting a new procedure provide for a trial period after which you will take suggestions and feedback

Brainstorming at Work

When you're working on a project and you hit a stumbling block, a great way to take some off you and to come up with the answer is to brainstorm. Some keys to keep in mind during a brainstorming session are:

> Write down each and every idea.
> Do not evaluate or criticize ideas during the session.
> Have a leader to keep the meeting on track.
> Have a set ending time. Consider using a timer, the pressure can work well. People tend to challenge themselves to see how many ideas they can come up with before the bell rings.
> Build off each other's suggestions.
> Use a large wipe board or paper so you don't limit yourself with the idea that "once the paper is full I'm done."

Your Briefcase or Laptop Bag

When you're considering buying a particular briefcase, ask yourself whether or not this is the right type for you. Is it the right size? Can you fit everything into it? Will you have more space left over than you need? Does it have lots of pockets that you could lose items in, or are there not enough compartments so everything gets jumbled together? There are many types of briefcases available. Choose one you'll use and enjoy having.

Do you carry your laptop with you? If so, do you have a separate bag for that? Do you really need to carry both bags or can you condense everything into one? Do you prefer a soft case or a hard one? Do you want a bag with a shoulder strap or one that only has a handle?

You might consider buying a computer bag that doesn't look like the traditional laptop bag to lessen the chances of theft.

Once you have chosen a briefcase or bag it's important to fill it with the right supplies. What have you been carrying in your briefcase or bag? Do you use everything you carry around, or can some of it be left behind? You want to limit number of supplies you carry with you. But make sure you have everything you need.

Decide what pockets will be used to hold what. Everything must have a home. Make sure there's enough room so the fit isn't too tight. Otherwise you can have trouble getting an item out. On the other hand, if the fit is too loose, the items may slide out. Which pocket does your cell phone slip into easily? Where will you put a few pens and maybe a highlighter? Do you want to carry Post-it notes or a memo pad? What else do you find yourself reaching for? Make sure you have that in your briefcase. Keep at least one envelope for receipts (if your job requires it).

Note: It's much easier to take a few minutes once a day to organize your briefcase or bag, rather than taking hours to do this task at the end of the week.

Business Cards and Contacts
In the future, you want to be able to locate contact information or file new information in a flash. To never again have to search for a scrap of paper that holds a phone number or look at a business card and wonder where it came from. Instead of having scattered pieces of paper everywhere choose one way of handling them. Two options

are a paper Rolodex type system or a computerized contact database.

The first thing to do is to figure out how you remember people. Some of us remember them by their first or last name. Others can recall the company name more quickly, and still others more readily recall the type of business. Whichever is true for you, that is the approach you should use to store the business cards and names in a contact database. Choose one way to recall the contacts and file their information alphabetically using that approach.

It is important to keep your contacts current. Have a small box on your desk where you can toss the weeks worth of contacts then enter them all Friday afternoon or delegate the task to someone else. Weed out old contacts routinely. Print the list and make changes to paper then delete when you have time or delegate the task to your assistant.

Clutter at the Office

The Wall Street Journal has stated that the average executive loses six weeks a year retrieving misplaced items. Based on a salary of $100,000, a company loses about $12,500 for each executive in lost time!

Clutter is stuff that is not in its home. It most commonly comes about for one of the following reasons.

- ➢ It was never given a home.
- ➢ You're postponing the decision of what to do with it.
- ➢ The item is mixed in with unrelated things.
- ➢ More than one item was left out because a project is unfinished.

Luckily there are two simple ideas you can keep in mind about clutter at work. First, do it now. Secondly, "when in doubt, throw it out." These basic ideas can help you make headway with the clutter.

"You can't have it all, where would you put it?"

It helps to make a decision about how long you're going to keep items. The Retention Schedule in the Appendix can be helpful in this regard. Let's look at one problem area now – periodicals. It helps to make a decision about how long you're going to keep items. Are they no longer useful after one month? Three months? Then recycle them. And recycle them even sooner if you can get the information off the Internet, from a co-worker or at the library.

Have a large garbage can that's easy to reach, does not have a lid and is emptied often.

File papers with a destroy date on them in red. Weed often.

Do you hesitate using the idea of "when in doubt, throw it out!" If you're uncomfortable with actually getting rid of things, then try and alternative mentioned earlier in this book. Box up the items and tape the box shut. Place a toss date on the box (three to six months in the future). Note the toss date on your calendar. If by that date, you have not used the things in the box, toss the whole box, without opening it to look at the contents.

There are both financial and emotional benefits of clearing out clutter. You save money because you see what you have and then don't have to buy a duplicate. You also have to spend a lot less money on storage. You're clearer about what you need to do so you can accomplish your goals and make money. Additionally, your stress is reduced so you feel calmer and more in control. You can find things and you don't have the overwhelming feeling that there's not enough time to do things.

In addition to physical clutter, there's also mental clutter -- things that are in your head that you keep trying to remember. An example is keeping a list of things to do in your head. When there's mental clutter you cannot think as clearly, you have trouble remembering things, and you feel stressed out. So do you want to think more clearly and feel less stressed? Then try what I call the brain drain. It works like this: You sit down with a pad of paper and you write down anything and everything that comes to mind. In the beginning simple items like take out the garbage, go to the bank and mail the bills may flood your mind. That's fine write down *everything*. Once you clear your mind of the minor items larger things will come to you. The idea is to get it all down on paper so that it is no longer in your head. Trying to remember it all is tough. But by writing it down you can clear your mind. This allows you to be more creative, freer and more open. Put the brain drain to practice at least once a week, this will help you feel less stressed.

Your Work Computer and Computer Files
Having to recreate files that have been lost is a definite minute muncher. You can lose files by not remembering where you put them or if they weren't backed up and the system crashes. Both of these problems are easy to combat. First, be sure you have anti-virus software up and running that updates often. Second, your computer should be set to auto backup or you can manually back it up. Third, give files meaningful names. File them in folders that make sense to you. Think of storing computer files just like you would store paper files in a filing cabinet. The drive is the

place where they are stored (like a cabinet or desk drawer), then the folder is the hanging folder where the inside manila folder will sit. Finally, the manila folder is the same as the title of the document.

If you are unable to locate a document you saved try the "find" option on your computer. This allows you to type in keys words that appear in the document and the computer will search its contents looking for files that match. One of the matches should be the file you are looking for.

Thirty to forty percent of all recorded information in the average organization is unnecessary duplicate copies of records that are maintained elsewhere within the organization.

If your job requires you to use a computer, then you're probably familiar with the most common functions a computer can perform -- like checking your spelling on a document or putting in page numbers. In addition to the basic functions, there are more advanced ones that can be extremely helpful. It only takes a little time to learn how to use them, and once you do, they can save you unbelievable amounts of time. Try some of the following:

Word Processing
There are many features that almost all word processing programs offer. There are options such as auto correct, undo and cut and paste that can save you a lot of time and aggravation. Take some time to familiarize yourself with the features your word processing offers.

Computer files
Here are two quick tips to ensure that you're able to locate files easily. First, delete old files. Second, place the number

one in front of commonly used files. That way, they will appear first on the list of files when you go to open one. Also, create templates for commonly typed documents and letters. Leave commonly used files, like fax cover sheets, open on your computer desktop during the day. That way when you need to send a fax you can quickly fill in the blanks and print one out.

Calendar

Here are three tips for those using an electronic calendar. To help yourself stay on track you can set pop-up reminders or enter a recurring task only once. You can also set things up so you can see another's schedule to check their availability.

Fax/E-mail

One great timesaving measure is to have your faxes come directly to your computer terminal. You can turn on/off the e-mail notification that new mail has arrived, and there's even an option to automatically spell-check your e-mail before sending it out.

Consider the fact that at last count research showed the average corporate worker sends and receives over 175 messages between e-mails, voicemails memos and other documents per day.

Contacts/Address Book

Save time by using the find option. Enter key words, and your contact's information will be brought up. Every time you have to look up or get contact information from somewhere, enter it into your contacts to avoid having to look it up again.

Organizing Disks and CDs

Do not lose files you have saved on disks color code by subject or project (use labels or colored disks) Keep in an organizer, there is a wide variety of organizers available.

Critic at Work

You have great ideas all day long don't just push them off. Sometimes a voice or your critic as I like to call it, tries to talk you out of things. Your critic may want you to believe that you are not good enough, the ideas are dumb or no one will want to do it. But "fire" your critic. Refuse to listen, instead note your great ideas in a journal so you can refer back to them at a later date.

Have a Deadline at Work?

Consider using what I call the funnel effect to get that project done on time. Picture a funnel; they are big at the top and small at the bottom. Imagine your goal at the bottom of the funnel, one small point to work towards. Now imagine everything that has to go into the funnel to work down to reach your goal. If you start at your goal and work backwards up the funnel; listing what all needs to get done and by when. You will create a perfect picture that includes everything that needs to get done.

Delegating Office Work

Delegating is a great way to pass along tasks that you don't have the time to do. Some people are better at particular things than others; figure out what the people around you do well. Certain people are great typists or have a knack for organizing and filing. Pick willing and capable people, and then delegate these types of tasks to them. Just because you don't like the task, do not assume others won't too.

The idea that we can do it better or quicker is often a reason that we don't delegate a task. Or we think that it takes too much time to teach someone how to do it. However it's beneficial in the long run to delegate. The fact that someone else can do it better, more efficiently, or enjoys the task is a great reason to pass it on.

Figure out which tasks you do on a daily basis and choose the ones that others can do for you. It's important to delegate the complete job, explain why it's done, and what the results will be. Stress the importance of the job and any deadlines that may be in place. You must be clear and, especially the first few times, be available to answer questions and for support or coaching. When you accept the completed task, remember that credit should be given to the person who actually did the work.

By reevaluating your daily tasks every three months (note this in the organizer as a reminder), you'll see what new work has developed. Then you can delegate more effectively and keep yourself running as efficiently as possible.

Your Desk at the Office
Your desk is the control center of your office. Here are some simple ideas that, when implemented, will help your day flow smoothly and allow you to work as efficiently as possible.

> ➤ Keep your in-box off your desk and close to the door. This allows people to drop in items without interrupting you. Your in-box is different than your "to file" box or "to do" box. Use your in-box for the single purpose of receiving paperwork so you can determine what to do with it.
> ➤ To keep the top of your desk organized, limit the number of souvenirs, mementoes and photos you keep there. Having them on a nearby shelf works better. Have only essential items on your desk.
> ➤ One *desktop organizer* that suits your needs should be the only one you need. Choose one made for the type of items you use often. For example: One type

has spaces for paperclips, writing instruments and a holder for sticky notes. Having more than one or the wrong kind is just as bad as not having one at all.

➤ What are some of the essential items that belong on your desktop? These usually relate to the project you're currently working on plus your "to do" list, the phone, your computer, a calendar, a notepad, a pen, a pencil, a highlighter, a stapler, a ruler, a staple remover, a calculator, and tape. Depending on your specialty, you may also have job-specific items that you need out all the time.

➤ A *drawer organizer* helps keep items from jumbling together in a drawer. Each drawer should be used to hold certain kinds of items and only those items. For instance designate a single drawer for all your personal items. Remember there's no such thing as a junk drawer.

➤ Place trays for outgoing papers somewhere off your desk. You can use one four trays; items to be: (1) faxed, (2) copied, (3) mailed, and (4) sent to co-workers.

➤ Aside from your desk, it may be necessary for you to have a work area -- a large blank area where you can spread out, and work. The area should be kept clear except for the project you're currently working on. Put all other projects away when you're not working on them -- even if they're not finished.

➤ Take the last few minutes of each day to wrap up and straighten your desk and work area. You can also rework your "to do" list and pull files you'll need for the morning. That way you can start fresh the next day with a clean space for working.

➤ Keep commonly used papers in files that are easy to reach. Do you order out a lot? Keep the collection of take-out menus in a handy-to-reach file.

➤ Place your cell phone on the side of your desk in its re-charger so it's all charged up when you need it.

- Keep an assortment of cards for all occasions in a desk drawer. This eliminates both uncomfortable moments when you forgot to buy a card and a trip to the store.
- Don't use a bulletin board; they're catch-alls for all types of unnecessary and quickly outdated items.

Coopers and Lybrandt estimate that the average person has thirty-seven hours of unfinished work on his/her desk at any one time. In addition, the average person uses less than 20% of what they save and wastes 150 hours a year looking for misplaced information. For someone earning $50,000 a year that translates to a loss of $3,842.00 a year.

Disaster Recovery on the Job
Emergencies can happen at any time, and they can range in severity from losing your wallet to a fire that destroys the entire office and all its contents. The solution is to always be prepared to handle any emergency. Here are some tips that can help you be ready to handle just about anything that comes up.

- Identify all records and files that you would need to rebuild the business within twenty-four hours. These are the documents that need to be protected. Consider keeping copies somewhere off-site. Then designate someone to keep track of how and where the documents are stored and of updating them.
- Keep a database of all the clients' names and key information.
- Make a photocopy of the front and back of all the information in your wallet. Important documents to copy are things like your driver's license, health insurance card, Social Security card, credit cards and other important cards. This way, you'll have the

account numbers and phone numbers to call for a replacement.

➢ Have a fireproof file box or cabinet to store all-important documents.

➢ Back up your computer and keep the disks locked up in a fireproof case or off-site.

➢ Keep an alternate start-up disk in case of a hard drive crash.

➢ Make sure that you're running off surge protectors and not just plugging important equipment into the wall outlet.

➢ Keep a hard copy of the following and keep off-site:

- Employer name, address and phone number
- Insurance agent's names, phone numbers and addresses
- Alarm system information
- Physicians' names, phone numbers and addresses
- Priest's, Minister's or Rabbi's name, phone number and address
- Relatives' names, phone numbers and addresses
- Neighbors' and friends' names, phone numbers and addresses
- Attorneys names, phone numbers and addresses
- Social Security office address and phone number
- Utility companies' names, phone numbers and addresses
- Banks' and other financial institutions' names, addresses, phone numbers and your account numbers

Ninety percent of U.S. organizations in private business or industry that lost their records due to some type of disaster during the twenty-five-year period between 1970 and 1995 never opened their doors again!

Office e-mail

E-mail is a convenient and easy way to communicate. There are features that can make it even easier -- like using a signature. Instead of signing your name to each e-mail along with your contact information, you use the signature that is comprised of a few lines that you use at the end of all your e-mails. You could include your name, title, company name, phone numbers, fax number, website address and maybe your e-mail address. You can also add a tag line about what your company does. A signature may look something like this:

John Doe
Director of Sales
ABC Company
Phone: 908-555-1212
Cell: 908-555-4321
Fax: 908-555-1234
www.ABCcompany.com
"Let's go sell something."

Some of the other most useful e-mail features are:

> You can save unfinished e-mails as drafts. This allows you to get interrupted and not have to start over; it also gives you the chance to leave an e-mail open until you have information on all the points you need to cover. That way, you don't have to send multiple e-mails to the same person in one day.
> There is an automatic file feature that saves a copy of all your outgoing messages.
> You can sort incoming messages by subject, key word or author.
> There's an option to color code messages. You can use this to indicate the order of importance of the e-mails or to identify the subject or the sender.

- When sending a message that requires a one-word answer like a yes or no you can set voting buttons so the receiver only has to hit yes or no to respond.
- You can set the options to notify you when a message is received and/or read.

Here are some helpful hints for using e-mail:

- Schedule specific times during the day to check and send your e-mail. You can set a reminder in your calendar until you get in the habit.
- Turn your e-mail notification off. This keeps you from being interrupted every time a new e-mail arrives.
- Use folders to organize and file incoming and archived messages.
- Fill in the address book; this makes it much simpler to send e-mails.
- Delete old e-mails that are no longer needed.

Remember, e-mail is not private and once it's sent there's no getting it back.

When you're on-line, keep the following e-mail etiquette in mind:

- Upper case is the equivalent of yelling. Use upper case sparingly and only to emphasize a point.
- Keep e-mails concise and to the point.
- Type a meaningful subject line.
- Only flag an e-mail urgent when it truly is; use regular priority most of the time.
- Place your e-mail on auto responder when you're out of the office.

Your Work Goals

Your goals can be as simple as "finish writing that memo" to "try to get promoted to Division Manager." Whatever they are, it's important to review your goals often to keep them in mind and to make adjustments as they change.

Write your goals down. Daily goals are written on a "to do" list. Others should be on a goal sheet – including both the short and long term ones. Give the goals reasonable achievement dates.

Have personal and business goals. Some examples are leaving on time every Friday, taking your full lunch outside the office, and getting promoted to head of the department.

Goals should reflect *your* wishes and desires -- not those of someone else.

A survey by Day-Timers Inc. found that 65% of American workers listed spending more time with their families as a priority or goal in their lives.

Interruptions Throughout Your Workday

The average manager is interrupted every eight to nine minutes, that's seven times an hour. This equates to fifty-to-sixty per day. The average interruption takes five minutes, totaling about four hours or 50% of the average workday. Eighty percent of those interruptions are typically rated as "little value" or "no value," creating more than three hours of wasted time per day.

It's inevitable; someone at some time is going to have to interrupt you for something. However, you do have some control over what you allow to intervene. The following hints will immediately decrease the number of times you are disrupted:

- ➢ Hang a "Do Not Disturb -- Genius at Work" sign on your door handle while you're in the middle of a project that requires your full attention.
- ➢ If you have an open door policy, post the hours that you are available for open door issues.
- ➢ Hold a daily meeting on all open projects to answer questions and bring everyone up to speed.
- ➢ If someone stops by to chat or has a question, stand up. This not only indicates that you're busy, the conversation will also go quicker. Or you can offer to talk with them while you walk somewhere that you need to go.
- ➢ If you're interrupted at an inconvenient moment, let the person know a better time when they could come back to talk to you. That way, they'll have your full attention.
- ➢ Turn off your e-mail notification; this will stop you from being interrupted each and every time a message is sent to you.
- ➢ Shut off the phone ringer while working on a project that demands your complete attention. Allowing all your calls to go to voice mail provides you a block of uninterrupted time.

Conversely, you can also control who *you* interrupt and for what. For instance, when you walk into someone's office, notice if they have their head down and seem intent on what they're working on. Consider coming back or at least ask if you've picked a good time.

Arrive on time to meetings and bring what you need wherever you go. For instance, having a pen and paper with you at a meeting will prevent you from interrupting it to find these items.

Mail Processing on the Job

The average executive receives twelve pieces of unsolicited mail a day. That adds up to 225 pieces a month.

Have your assistant go through the mail the first time -- pulling out and discarding junk mail, then opening and dating other incoming mail. Also, your assistant should pull any files needed to respond to the other mail.

Then you go through your mail one time a day. Go through the mail near the garbage can and shredder. Also have your tickler file and organizer handy so you can jot down notes.

Business Meetings

The average manager spends seventeen hours a week in meetings.

When you're asked to attend a meeting, consider the following:

> - Review the agenda; do you really need to go? Can you send your assistant as your representative? Can you just read the minutes after?
> - Is there anything you need to prepare or bring with you?
> - Be sure to bring your planner and "to do" list so you can note deadlines and assignments.
> - Turn off your cell phone and/or pager.
> - Tell someone if there's a call you're expecting or anything else you should be interrupted for.
> - Arrive on time. If you're late, wait until a break to ask a co-worker what you missed.

Nine out of ten people daydream in meetings.

When you're facilitating a meeting, here are some points to consider:

- ➢ Does the meeting have to be done in person or will a teleconference be a better choice?
- ➢ Is a meeting the best possible way to disseminate the information? Would a broadcast voicemail or group e-mail be a smarter approach?
- ➢ If the meeting will be brief, conduct it standing up. It'll be less formal and things will go faster.
- ➢ Be sure to start and end on time. If you need more time, schedule a follow-up meeting.
- ➢ Have designated "open door" hours with times clearly posted, to discuss the meeting beforehand and afterwards.
- ➢ Only invite the necessary people to attend; the less people, the faster the meeting will go.
- ➢ Prior to the meeting, pass out written agendas with a time frame for each topic to be discussed. Place the start time and the end time on the agenda. And note in bold type if someone is responsible for bringing something to the meeting.
- ➢ Designate someone as the timekeeper; this person will also be responsible for keeping the meeting on track. Rotate this duty from meeting to meeting.
- ➢ Make someone responsible for taking notes and distributing them within 48 hours of the meeting. Make sure action items are noted in bold.
- ➢ Bring your planner and "to do" list so you can note deadlines and "to do" items.
- ➢ Have everyone stand and stretch every thirty minutes. Attention spans are about that long.
- ➢ At the start of the meeting, request that everyone turn off his/her cell phones and turn pagers to vibrate.

➤ Schedule a brief ten-minute meeting with someone if you need his or her time and it's more than just a quick question.

➤ Add a question and answer period at the end of the meeting. Let people know it's coming so they'll save all their questions until then. Most likely, their questions will be answered sometime during the remainder of the meeting.

➤ Should someone have a very specific question, ask to speak with them one-on-one after the meeting.

➤ Institute a brief, standing ten-minute daily meeting with all those involved on a particular project. All questions can be asked at this time and instructions can be clarified. This time can be used to bring everyone up to speed on the project. This practice allows you to answer questions once so everyone can hear the answers and it eliminates a lot of miscommunication.

➤ At the end of the meeting recap, what was discussed and who is responsible for what.

➤ Schedule the next meeting, if necessary.

On the average day, there are 17 million meetings in America.

If you don't like attending the group's meetings, then resign from the group.

Professional Networking
Referrals can come from many sources. One of the most valuable and reliable are referrals through direct contact -- like meeting someone at a conference or having someone approach you after you've given a lecture. Here are some networking pointers:

- Join an association; be selective about the one you pick. Make sure it suits your needs. It's better to join one and spend time getting to know people there rather then joining many associations and spreading yourself too thin.
- Be the first to arrive at functions; fashionably late does not work for networking. Get there early; greet people coming in who look like first-timers. Or mingle near the refreshments as people arrive and get themselves a drink.
- Volunteer to work the nametag table; it's an easy way to meet people and to ask what they do.
- Go with twenty-five of your business cards in one pocket; make a deal with yourself not to leave until you have given them all out.
- Set a goal of collecting x number of cards before you leave the event.
- Write key information on the back of the cards that you collect. Put the date; note what you talked about and any other important information.
- Remember: you only get one chance to make a first impression; make it a good one.
- Create and memorize a thirty-second commercial that you can rattle off when someone asks you what you do.
- During the conversation, you can say, "These are the people who I work with..." and name the type of people who are your best clients/customers.
- Practice small talk.
- Read up on the day's events and other current events before you go.

Other tips are:

- On the back of your business card have something people would need to refer to often (like a calendar or tipping chart). That way they will pull out your card often.

➤ Send people non-business related notes to let them know you're thinking of them. For example, say you meet someone who might be a potential client. They mention that they're going on a family vacation to France. After meeting them, you come across something in the paper about France, send it to the person with a note wishing them a good trip or welcoming them back from their vacation.

➤ Always carry business cards no matter where you go. Some great networking can take place in line at the grocery store or at the gym.

Your Paper Filing System at Work

Before you can set up a filing system, you have to decide what you'll be keeping. Remember that 80% of what's filed is never referenced again. Please see the Retention Schedule in the Appendix in the back of the book.

In a recent survey by Steelcase, 27% of office workers described themselves as "pilers." Twelve percent called themselves "pack rats."

An Ernst & Young study revealed that it costs $2,100 a year to maintain a filing cabinet. An average of thirty-seven of the documents are lost or misfiled; recovering them costs $120 per document.

You need an easy filing system. Remember: if it's easy, you'll use it. If you need a map to figure out what drawer the file belongs in then let's be honest -- you won't file it. Here are some filing tips:

➤ File the most recent items in the front. That way, you don't have to flip through entire file to read most recent information in it.

167

- Insert file tabs on front of file as opposed to the back or can't read the tab when the file starts to get filled.
- Use 3 ½" not 2" tabs. The smaller tabs are harder to read or you have to abbreviate and then you don't know what's in the file.
- Use upper and lower case. We read that faster then when it's all in one case.
- Have all the files you use regularly within arms' reach. Think about trying a rolling cart.
- Use label names that mean something to you.
- Use a noun, not words like "other" or "miscellaneous."
- Group "like things" together (all financial, all clients, etc.) then file alphabetically within that group. Consider color-coding.
- Use hanging folders with broad topics like "Telephones." Then put manila file folders inside them. For our example you'd have a manila folder for each telephone -- cell, home and car.
- A file is only effective if you can retrieve it again.
- There are four types of files -- archive, current, reference and tickler.
- Have a shallow tray off your desk where you can toss all the folders that need to be filed.
- Never overload files or the drawers; leave room for adding papers to existing files and for new files.
- Staple or use a binder clip to group papers within a file. Don't use paper clips, they tend to catch other papers.
- Schedule time to file or delegate to your assistant.
- Use color-coding if you remember colors easily. However, don't choose odd colors that may be discontinued or out-of-stock when you need them.
- Use clear tabs on colored files; they're easier to read.
- Label the manila folders inside the hanging folder with the hanging folders' name so you'll know

where they belong. This makes re-filing much easier.

> Use red pen and write a destroy date on the manila folders.
> Place a destroy date on boxes of archived files.
> Set up twenty-five blank files that are ready to use.
> Use 3 tab instead of 5 tab manila folders. They have a larger space to write on so you don't have to abbreviate.
> Try the following method instead of placing the tabs on the hanging folders all the way across (and then have to move them when you add a new file.) For all files that start with the letters A-G, insert their tab on the left side, all files H-P get their tab inserted in the center slot. For the files Q-Z get their tab stuck on the right-hand side of the hanging folder.

According to the American Demographic Society, Americans waste more than 9 million hours each day looking for lost and misplaced articles.

The average American employee uses 250 pounds of paper every year.

Phone Calls on the Job

Take control of your phone; don't let the phone control you. There are tips that can cut down on your phone time considerably – if you implement them. First, choose a two-hour window in which you will make and receive most of your calls. List this time span on your voice mail so people will know when to expect your call. The two hours right before or after lunch or before the end of the day seem to work well because people are more likely to be in the office, available and less chatty. If you know a person to be particularly chatty, then start your call off with "I only have a minute but I wanted to call...."

Other ideas that can shave minutes off your phone time are:

> Get the persons' direct dial number in case you ever need to call back. That way, you can get right through.
> Ask the person if they have a pen before you start rattling off important information like phone numbers and addresses. Request that they repeat what you had them write down.
> Have a pen and paper handy whenever you pickup the phone.
> Planned calls take much less time than unplanned calls. Make sure you write down everything you want to cover ahead of time, this avoid having to call back to cover missed points.
> Make a list of talking points for the call and cross them off as they're covered.
> Take notes while on the phone and have your planner handy to jot down "to do" items and dates.
> Start any call you make by asking the person if it's a good time to talk.
> Turn the ringer off during tasks that require your full attention.

And lastly, for the time that you do need to spend on the phone, be kind to your neck and use a hands-free device.

Project Management
Work projects have a way of sucking up your time. By managing them more closely you'll waste less time. Here are some great ways to get a handle on your projects:

> Assume the project will take longer than you think it actually will. That way, you'll be sure to finish ahead of schedule. Or if you run long, you'll still

170

have it done on time. This is called "under-promising and over-delivering"; it will always make you look good.

➢ Before beginning a project, hold a brainstorming session to get all the ideas and angles about it before you begin.

➢ Utilize time-savers like templates. Refer back to similar projects for ideas so you don't have to keep reinventing the wheel.

➢ Maintain open lines of communication with all those involved with the project. When delegating a task have the person repeat back what they're going to do and what they heard you say. That way, you can correct any miscommunications at the start. Get continual status updates by holding regular, quick, informal, stand-up staff meetings that include only the people directly involved on the project.

➢ Lastly, work on a project during your prime time. That's the time of day when you're best suited to be doing the job. For example: If you're just so-so when it comes to dealing with numbers, do a numerical project during the time when you're most alert and focused and have the most patience.

Procrastination at the Office

Typically, procrastination involves something that needs to be done now that you're postponing for some reason. It occurs at the office as well as at home.

Some common thoughts that cause procrastination:

➢ "I'll do it when I'm in the mood."
➢ "I'll start tomorrow."
➢ "There's plenty of time to get it done."
➢ "I don't know where to begin."
➢ "I work better under pressure."
➢ "It won't turn out perfect, so why start."

171

➢ "I enjoy the rush and pressure of waiting until the last minute."
➢ Worrying over the project.

Other reasons it occurs:

➢ Fear.
➢ A habit of delaying decisions.
➢ You don't really want to do it.
➢ You're too busy to do it.

Here are some ways to get over it and get the job done:

➢ Break up large, unmanageable projects into smaller, more doable ones.
➢ Set limits. Use a timer and do as much as you can in a set amount of time.
➢ Give yourself a reward for doing something you really didn't want to do.
➢ First thing in the morning, tackle that one project which has been looming overhead. That way, nothing else that day will be as unpleasant.
➢ Can you delegate this or hire it out?
➢ Adopt a "do it now" philosophy.

Work-related Reading
At the office unread magazines, business reports and other material build up in a reading pile. You mean to get to it, but the uninterrupted time never seems to be there. There are a few quick fixes to eliminate the reading pile. First, you have to clear away the pile you already have. Then simply manage incoming reading material as you receive it, and the reading pile will never build up again!

Take a look at what's in your reading pile now. Are there items you subscribe to? Are there more than two months' worth? If so, consider canceling the subscription. You can always re-subscribe later.

As you go through the pile, ask yourself, "Do I have time to read this?" and "do I really want to read this?" If either answer is "no," dump it. If the information will be out-of-date by the time you get to read it, toss it. Is there another way you can get the information if you need it -- like through the Internet, from a co-worker, or at a library? If so, recycle the items. As you continue to sift through your reading pile, scan the contents pages and pull out any articles if it's of interest to you. Staple the article together and place it in a file that you have labeled "to read." Carry this file with you when you're likely to have to wait, like in a doctor's office or at the vet. Have a highlighter with you as you read the articles. That way, if you want to file them, you can simply highlight the word that you will file it under.

It will be important that you schedule time in your calendar to read. If you wait to pencil the time in, there will be no time left. Pick a day and time on a weekly basis that's good and plan to read for thirty minutes to an hour. This will stop the reading pile from building again to unmanageable heights.

Office Ergonomics

Keep in mind that no one workstation fits all. Just as you need to adjust exercise equipment before working out, you may need to make adjustments to your workstation. Maybe your neck is sore by the end of the day or your fingers cramp up while you're typing. What do you need to change? Here are some guidelines for creating a worker-friendly workstation:

Computer:
  - ➢ Keep the computer dust-free.
  - ➢ Consider using an anti-glare screen.
  - ➢ Your eyes should be 24-36" away from the screen.

➤ Make sure the type size you work with is legible on the screen. You can type in a large font and reduce it before printing.
➤ Use a document holder when typing from a document.
➤ Make sure the mouse is within reach; you shouldn't have to stretch for it.

Posture
➤ Have your neck bent at a 15° angle, either up or down.
➤ Fingers should be slightly curved upward so the keying motion is gentle and comfortable.
➤ The back of your shoulders should be relaxed and in a natural position.
➤ Sit firmly in the chair with your back against the back of your chair.
➤ Your elbows should be on the armrests and at a 90° angle.
➤ Your knees should be bent at a 90° angle.
➤ Make sure your feet are planted securely on the floor or a footrest.

Lighting
➤ Check the overhead lighting. Are any of the bulbs burned out or flickering?
➤ Consider full-spectrum bulbs that duplicate sunlight.
➤ Utilize task lighting, like a desk lamp.
➤ Allow natural light to brighten the room, without causing a glare.

Office and Workstation
➤ Use a hands-free headset for the telephone.
➤ Keep the office temperature between 68° to 74.5°. Use a portable heater or a fan if necessary.

- ➢ Plug in a white noise machine or another soothing sound machine to cover office noise.
- ➢ Consider using an air purifier.
- ➢ A rock garden and water fountain enhance the atmosphere by providing a relaxing gentle flow of water in the background.
- ➢ Set a timer or a reminder in your calendar/organizer to prompt you to take a break every twenty minutes. Be sure to look away from the monitor, close your eyes, gaze into the distance, or blink a lot. You can use natural tears for extra moisture. Also, allow yourself a few minutes to get up and walk around. This is a good time to go make copies or fax documents.

Self-management on the Job

With so much going on around us, it's very easy to get distracted from what we really need to be focusing on. Here are a few tips to help keep you on track:

- ➢ Use only one calendar or organizer. More than one creates chaos.
- ➢ Make appointments with yourself to do things you enjoy.
- ➢ Start to schedule time for moving toward those "I'll get around to them dreams." What have you been waiting to get to? Whatever it is, start making progress towards it. If your dream is a vacation then start a vacation fund and create a file where you can place clippings about places to go.
- ➢ Use a timer during projects. You're much more likely to pay attention to how long something is taking you if you have a clock ticking off the minutes. And it usually will not take you as long to do something with a timer as without.
- ➢ Figure out how much your time is worth. For example, if you make $40,000 a year, then an hour

of your time is worth about $19.23. Spend your $19 wisely.

> Keep your focus during a project. While you're involved with one project stick with it. If you remember something about another task, write it down on your "to do" list and take care of it later. Don't stop doing what you're doing to take care of other things; you may get so sidetracked that you might never get to finish what you started.

Job Stress
Do you relate to any of the following statements?

> I have trouble getting up in the morning.
> I often feel tired.
> I forget things.
> I have unexplained aches and pains.
> I often have headaches and/or stomachaches.
> I lose my temper quickly.
> I feel overwhelmed most of the time.
> I watch the clock at work.

Most of us can benefit from taking steps to reduce our work stress. If you related to the statements above, make a special effort to reduce your stress on the job. Here are some ideas to get you started:

> Take at least two fifteen minute breaks.
> Don't eat at your desk.
> Breathe deeply often.
> Take vitamins.
> Drink fresh fruit or veggie juice.
> Move your body.
> Learn self-massage.
> Drink lots of water.
> Use lavender or another oil in a diffuser.
> Relax your mind.
> Try positive visualization.

176

- ➤ Exercise at least twenty minutes every day.
- ➤ Let go, you can't do it all or control everything.
- ➤ Make your "to do" list short and achievable.
- ➤ Congratulate yourself on your successes.
- ➤ Share the load; delegate.
- ➤ Make time for things other than work.

Making some simple changes can reduce the amount of stress you feel. Take a look at your work environment; is it pleasant? For example, do you work in a cubicle that has gray panel alls and a drab rug? Think of ways that you can dress it up. Consider bringing in a few potted plants; green plants can liven up any area. Put up meaningful pictures or posters. Hang a mobile or wind chimes. Listen to what's going on around you. Is there a lot of distracting noise coming from office machinery or nearby co-workers? Consider playing nature sound tapes or CDs or have a tabletop fountain running in the corner of your desk. You can even put down a small colorful carpet or an oriental rug; either will brighten up the area and make it more inviting. You can also bring in a few fun items like Silly Putty, search-a-word books, crossword puzzles, a snow globe or magnetic puzzles; any of these items are great to kid around with at break time.

Plan fun activities with your family or friends after-work hours. This gives you something to look forward to during your workday.

Seventy-five percent of American workers complain that they're tired.

Office Tickler File
This is used for items that will require some sort of action in the future. It's quite possibly one of the most useful of all the organizing tools. However, the only way the tickler

file will work is if it's checked each and every day -- no exceptions!

The tickler file is very easy to set up and to maintain. It requires forty-three folders, hanging folders or an accordion file work well. Label the first group with the numbers one through thirty-one and then label the rest, one for each month of the year. Now put them in a convenient place -- a desk drawer, a freestanding file or rolling file somewhere in the office. It's your choice.

Now you're ready to start using your tickler file; it's that easy! Say someone hands you an agenda for a meeting next Friday the 12th. Place the agenda in the 11th file. On Thursday the 11th, you'll open the file and be reminded of the meeting the next day. You can review the agenda to see if there's anything you need to prepare to bring to the meeting. Then place the agenda and whatever you need to bring into the 12th file. That way it will be waiting for you in the morning. Never again will you overlook a meeting or forget to bring something with you that you need.

Another example: You receive an invitation to a holiday party and you need to buy a grab-bag gift. The invitation says to RSVP by a certain date. Put the invitation in the RSVP day's file. On that day, you'll be reminded to respond. Then you can also place an order for the grab-bag gift. Now place the invitation in the file of the day you expect the gift to arrive. In addition, you may want to note the gift item, the phone number of the company, how you paid, and the order number. Then when you pull out the invite again, you'll be reminded that the gift should have arrived. If it has not, you can call and check on the order status. Or if the gift was delivered, you can file the invitation under the day before the party in the tickler file.

Until you get used to using the tickler file, you may find it helpful to jot the letter "T" down next to the item when you write it in your organizer. That will remind you the information about it is in the tickler file. Also, you may find it helpful to rotate files so the current date is always in front. Have the tickler file handy when you're opening the mail and sorting through your in-box.

Time Management at Work
You have a limited amount of time each day. Here are some areas where time can easily be lost and some ideas to keep it from happening.

Projects
> - A common mistake is underestimating the amount of time a project will actually take.
> - Assume projects will take longer than you think.
> - Under-promise; over-deliver.
> - Hire out or delegate projects.
> - Make sure that you have all the tools before you begin. You don't want to print a presentation and then have no cover to put it in.
> - Finish what you start. If you think of something in the middle, write it down and come back to it later.
> - Remember the job will expand to fill amount of time allotted.
> - Maintenance versus an emergency. An emergency costs more and takes more time.

Visitors
> - Stand up; the meeting will go faster.
> - Have no extra chairs or keep chairs far away from your desk.
> - Walk and talk.
> - Don't look up as people pass your office; it's an invitation for them to stop in.

Prime Time
  - ➢ Are you at your best in the morning, afternoon or evening?
  - ➢ Do the task at the right time of day for you.
  - ➢ Non-thinking tasks can be done at low-energy times.
  - ➢ Intricate projects should be done at high-energy times.

I once worked with a client who worked in an office as a general assistance. She was assigned projects as they came up. She might be assigned a spreadsheet for the finance department, a presentation for the marketing department and a letter from the vice-president all in one day. She enjoyed the variety in her day and the opportunity to use many of her skills, however she would often find herself struggling over a complex spreadsheet mid-afternoon or having difficulty starting letters early in the morning. We discussed the idea of prime time and making the best use of your energy. We realized that she felt most creative later on in the day, after she got settled into the work for the day, the ideas started to flow. And she was best able to concentrate on figures and data early in the morning before she has tons of things going on. So she retooled her workday to get spreadsheets and other projects that required a lot of concentration out of the way in the morning. Then she could delve into the more creative projects, like composing letters, in the afternoon.

Appointments and Errands
  - ➢ Don't overbook.
  - ➢ Have one place to write all of your appointments.
  - ➢ Pad time around appointments.
  - ➢ Confirm all appointments before leaving the office.

- Confirm your in-office appointments too.
- Utilize cancellation time wisely, it's "found time."
- Book the first appointment of day or the first after lunch. Appointments run father behind as the day passes.
- Do tasks at logical times. For example, don't go to the bank on Friday or Monday (common paydays) or between 11:30 AM - 1:30 Pm (lunch time).

Commute
- Use books on tape
- Work/read while on a bus or a train
- Carry a mini-tape recorder to tape your thoughts when writing is not convenient (like while driving).
- Utilize a hands-free cell phone device.
- Make sure you allow extra time when traveling. This enables you to be early and to settle in before starting work. Also, factors in time for unexpected events like construction and accidents.

Tied up in traffic coming to and/or leaving from work? Avoid sitting in long lines by adjusting your start by. By simply starting work ten to fifteen minutes earlier or later you can significantly lessen your commute.

Calendar/Schedule
- It *must* have some white space.
- Schedule time to do things like read.
- Schedule "your time" first and in pen.
- Schedule planning time.

181

- ➤ Take fifteen minutes at the end of your weekday to wrap up. Clear off your desk and work area. Pull files you'll need and prepare for your morning and by reviewing your next days calendar.
- ➤ At home, get ready for the day the night before. Set the table for breakfast; locate your keys and briefcase, etc.
- ➤ Remember, sleep depravation is a major time-waster.

Procrastination
- ➤ When you can, avoid taking a job you don't want or won't know what to do with.
- ➤ The anticipation is worse then actually doing the task.
- ➤ Break up large jobs into smaller tasks and get started.
- ➤ Delegate.
- ➤ Hire out.

Organized Movement
- ➤ Get up once to get coffee, make copies, stamp a letter, fax, etc.
- ➤ Tell people to expect your fax around X time, that way you can get up once to send all your faxes.
- ➤ Every time you get up for something, pay attention to what it is. If it's commonly used all the time or just for this project, consider keeping it closer -- like placing the files in a rolling crate.
- ➤ Do "like tasks" together.
- ➤ See what services offer free pickup and delivery, like office supplies, dry cleaning, printer and car wash, etc.

> Keep an assortment of greeting cards on hand, including blank ones, to avoid running out to the card shop.

The Clock
> Wear a watch.
> Leave work on time. Consider having a co-worker who leaves on time stop to walk out with you.

Tasks
> Do things well, not perfectly.
> Establish deadlines.
> Use a timer.
> Adopt a "do it now" mentality.
> One in, one out. Take on a new task; delete another task.

Interruptions
> Utilize a "Do not Disturb. Genius at work" sign.
> Turn off the ringer for your phone and the e-mail notification.

Tips
> Program speed-dial on the phone, fax, etc.

People Pages
> Write down everything you need to discuss with a person. Then compose one memo or e-mail, leave one voice mail, or go to see them once.

Saying no
> If you say yes, what are you saying no to? A night at home with family?
> Saying "no" is the single most effective time-management tool.

> Don't like to say no? Want to help? Feel obligated? Don't want to disappoint? Think you'll wish you said yes later? Well, you can usually say yes another time.

The average person uses thirteen different methods to control and manage their time.

Fifty-two percent of American workers mentioned their job as the reason they're unable to spend more time with their spouse.

Your "To Do" List on the Job
You can't do something if you don't remember that it needs to be done, so you need a "to do" list that's written down instead of kept in your head. And it's important not to confuse the "to do" list with the wish I had time to-do list. These are two separate and distinct lists. The to-do list is made up of the five to ten tasks that you actually plan to do that day. They can be sorted by category or by priority. The "wish I had time to do" list is the list where all those others things get written down. All those things you mean to get to, you hope you'll have time for, but somehow you never do.

It will give you a sense of satisfaction each and every time you complete a task and can cross it off your "To Do" list.

The fact is that scheduling too many things in too little time guarantees chaos, inefficiency, ineffectiveness and failure. No one likes to fail, so set yourself up to succeed.
When you do one task, it may create another one that needs to be done. For example: When you finish entering all the data, you may now need to run a report.

Here are some tips for managing your "To Do" list and the items on it.

- ➢ Don't prioritize your schedule; schedule your priorities.
- ➢ Carry the "To Do" list with you; add to it as needed.
- ➢ Update the list daily or at night as you prepare for morning.
- ➢ Break up large projects. It is a large project of you need more than an hour to finish it.
- ➢ Delegate.
- ➢ Hire out.
- ➢ Cross off/check off as done.
- ➢ Take time to respond.
- ➢ Stop justifying why you can't and just say you can't.
- ➢ A to do basket is not the same as in basket or today basket.
- ➢ If your today basket is not empty at the end of the day, you're planning too much.
- ➢ If your in box is not empty at end of day you are using it wrong.
- ➢ Send group e-mails and voice mails when appropriate. Set up different groups of recipients ahead of time.

A survey by Day-Timers Inc. found that 62% of American workers feel they are always or frequently rushed to do the things they have to do.

Tolerances
We all tolerate some things related to our jobs; tolerations are those annoying things that we all live with. However, maybe something can be done about them -- or at least a good many of them. The first step is to identify what you're tolerating at work. Give yourself time to make a really good list and be as specific as possible. Items on your list

185

might be as large as "my car breaks down too often on the way to and from my job" to something more trivial like "I have a ton of pens, but few actually write."

Think about all the things that make you sigh when you encounter them. If you often open your briefcase and can't find the papers you need, this zaps you of your energy. You feel bad that you haven't done something about it and you anticipate all the time it's going to take to fix.

The irony is that the energy you must expend to tolerate these things is far more than the energy you would need to fix them. But it's usually finding the time that stops us from doing something about them. That's why creating this list is a great start; the next step is to actually begin chipping away at the tolerations related to your work. But first, review the list and put the items in order of importance. Once you have your list sorted in order of priority you can start the real work of making the changes so that your work life contains as few tolerations as possible.

Look at each item and think of a way to resolve it. No ink in the majority of your pens? Then the next time you're on the phone, take a sheet of paper and test the pens; toss those without ink. And if you're left with only a few pens, place an order for a box or two to be delivered. And you might consider speaking with a mechanic about the repairs expected on your car in the near future and plan to make only the necessary repairs for the next twelve months, while you set aside money on a monthly basis for a down payment on a new car. Have your planner with you while you go over your list, some of the larger items may require time and/or planning. Big items may need to be broken up into small tasks. You might block out an hour or two to handle an item such as drawing up a new way to organize you office or you might call in a Professional Organizer for a consultation and ideas or to actually do the work. Taking some sort of action will begin to relieve your frustration.

Simply moving towards eliminating things that annoy you is very liberating!

Traveling for Your Job

Preparing to travel can be stressful; the following are some ideas to keep you on track while you're preparing to leave, packing and then later dealing with the backlog when return. (See the Master Packing List in the Appendix.)

<u>**Packing Tips**</u>

> Designate one place to gather all the receipts you'll collect on the trip.

> Take comfortable clothes for any spare time you may end up with.

> Is there a gym or a pool in the hotel? Will you need a bathing suit or exercise clothes?

> Call ahead to see what the hotel provides – like an iron, razor, coffee machine, and hairdryer -- to avoid over-packing.

> Go to your bathroom; make a list of everything you use, then get travel sizes.

> Coordinate outfits so that you can use certain pieces more than once. Example: One black skirt and pants with different tops and blazers.

> Choose your outfits for each day and write them downs

> Designate a single packing place where only things that are going with you will be placed.

> Put anything that may leak in a plastic bag.

> If you need to pack items you'll be using the day you're leaving make a list and check them off as you pack them at the last minute.

> Pack your laptop in a sturdy case that's not a computer case to lessen the chances of theft.

> If you're traveling with someone from your household, pack each bag with half of their clothes and half of yours. That way, if one bag is lost, you

both have a change of clothes and at least one complete outfit.

➢ Carry as much as possible onto the plane to avoid the possibility of it getting lost.
➢ Verify current safety regulations that are in place so you can sail through baggage checks and not have anything confiscated by security.
➢ Make sure that you pack vital items in your carry-on (prescription medication, spare glasses, etc.).
➢ Roll your clothes for packing; it saves space and does not crease them when done right.
➢ Put socks inside shoes to avoid flattening your footwear.
➢ Place belts around the inside wall of the suitcase to avoid rolling them and possibly damaging the material.
➢ Make sure that the ID tags have the final destination on them.
➢ Attach strips of distinctive material to the handle of each of your bags so that your bags are easy for you to identify.
➢ Put ID tags inside the bags in case the outside ID tag is lost.

Please refer to the Packing List located in the back of the book.

Before Leaving
➢ Cancel your newspaper.
➢ Put a hold on your mail.
➢ Change your answering machine messages.
➢ Schedule time in your calendar to deal with the backlog and what happened on the trip when you get back. Consider using the first day strictly for

catch-up and make your official day back your second day in the office.

- ➤ Give out house and office keys to trusted neighbors or family members.
- ➤ Forward e-mail or put on the auto responder.
- ➤ Buy and pack gifts, including one for your host.
- ➤ Designate a house sitter.
- ➤ Get a pet-sitter or turn on the automatic feeders.
- ➤ Put your lights on timers.
- ➤ Turn off your pager.
- ➤ Arrange for coverage of important projects or to field customer requests while you're away.
- ➤ Leave your day-by-day itinerary with co-workers, family and/or friends.
- ➤ Pre-pay bills that will come due while you're away.

When You Return
- ➤ Use your first day back to catch up and deal with what happened on the trip.
- ➤ Write any thank you notes that need to be written or send gift baskets.
- ➤ Hand in expense report and receipts.
- ➤ Write a report of the trip (if required).

Office Voice Mail
Voice mail is a great feature; it's most commonly used to take a message in your absence. But there's much more that voice mail is capable of. Here are some hints for getting the most out of your voice mail system and making other's voice mail work for you.

In your outgoing voice mail message:

- ➤ Ask the caller to leave a message explaining what they need. That way, you can get it to them without playing phone tag if they are away when you call back. This can prevent phone tag.

189

- State that you will be returning calls between X and Y time.
- Tell the caller what to do if they need assistance in the meantime.
- Give your fax number, web address and any other common requests.
- Ask the caller to leave the best time for you to get back to them.

When leaving a message on voice mail, you should:

- Speak slowly.
- Leave your phone number. You never know where they will be when picking up your message; they may not have your number handy.
- Include what you need in your message, so they can get it to you if you just need an answer. Also the chances are better that you'll get a return call if they know what you're calling about.
- Leave the date and time of your call.

Although voice mail may come in handy, it can become a time-waster if you check your voice mail every time it indicates that you have a message. Instead, get in the habit of checking your voice mail once in the morning and once in the afternoon.

And remember; when you're working on a project that demands your full attention, you should consider turning the ringer off or have someone else answer your line for that period of time. Just because the phone rings doesn't mean you have to answer it.

A balance can be made between your work life and your personal life. It will require that you make changes, identify priorities, and stick to your boundaries. Soon you'll have a smooth running system that allows you the time to handle

work during business hours and everything else will have
its place.

Chapter Highlights
- Concentrate on top priorities.
- Plan and take vacations.
- Limit minute munchers.
- Delegate.
- Avoid as many stressors as possible.
- Prepare for the day the night before.

Chapter Resources
- officemax.com 800-788-8080
- www.iaap-hq.org/ - International Association of
  Administrative Professionals (formerly Professional
  Secretaries International) - 816-891-6600
- assistu.com - 410-666-5900
- Life U Love – 1-866-294-9900
  369 Evergreen Blvd.
  Scotch Plains, NJ 07076
  www.lifeulove.com – jamie@lifeulove.com

Next figure out what you want and how to get it.
AKA Reaching for Your Dreams and Goals

This section is for you if any of the following apply:

➢ You break New Year's resolutions before January is over.

➢ There are things you've been meaning to accomplish that you never find time to work toward.

By the end of this chapter, you'll be able to:

➢ Set long-term goals and stay on track to meet them.

➢ Achieve what you set out to do.

➢ Have your goals in writing.

➢ Remember to review your goals often and update them as needed.

➢ Make and keep New Year's resolutions.

➢ Have your life go according to plan.

➢ Anticipate and plan ahead.

➢ Make list-making a part of your life.

Introduction

"What the mind of man can conceive and believe, it can achieve." Napoleon Hill

Goals and dreams -- those things we wish to accomplish "one of these days." But that day in the future is not going to just appear; we have to make it happen. Here are some pointers on reaching your goals and dreams.

A survey by Day-Timers Inc. found that 78% of the workforce mention getting more exercise as a goal. Sixty-five percent would like to spend more time with family, and 59% would like to eat better.

"If you can dream it, you can do it." Walt Disney

"A journey of a thousand miles begins with a single step." Chinese Proverb

You're First Steps

An important, initial step to reaching your goals and dreams is writing them down. Then watch how your words grow! You'll want to word your list carefully! For example, if you want to lose weight (the most popular goal of Americans), writing "lose weight" is not nearly as helpful as writing "eat healthy, exercise and take a class in nutrition." All of these things will get you to your goal of losing weight but they are *specific actions* that you can take.

Once you have your specific goals down on paper, you should review them to make sure that they are reasonable. For instance, if you write that you want to save $1,000 a week but you only make $500 a week, that is not a reasonable goal. I exaggerated this example to make the point that it is important that you assess the goal to make sure it's doable. No sense setting yourself up for failure by writing down goals that cannot be achieved.

Set Goal Dates

So you have your goals written out and you've made them specific. You know that even though they may be a stretch, you have a good chance of reaching them. The next step is attaching a date to them. This is a goal date by which you wish to have accomplished what you set out to do. Again, make sure that the time frame you set up is reasonable. It's better to say six months and get to it done in five than to say two months and have no real hope of achieving your goal by then. And sometimes you may find that you want to concentrate more on being satisfied with what you have than always looking to get something else. There's an old saying that goes like this: "Success is not getting what you want; it's wanting what you already have."

> *"The first step to getting the things you want out of life is this: Decide what you want."* Ben Stein

> *"Dream as if you'll live forever. Live as if you'll die today."* James Dean

Keep Moving Ahead

Now take it day by day. Make little steps towards achieving the big goals. Remember that it takes twenty-eight days to create a new habit. So that means you shouldn't expect to see changes immediately. Give yourself time to create new habits and keep in mind that every day is another chance to get on track.

Ninety percent of those who join health and fitness clubs will stop going within the first 90 days.

Sticking With Your Plan
It can sometimes feel overwhelming to think about your goals in the long term. For example: If you have a goal of saving X number of dollars by a certain date, you may feel guilty or resentful when you wish you could buy a new outfit. Feeling that way can lead to quitting your plan to reach your goal. Instead of allowing this to happen, try to look at your goal day by day. When you go a whole day without making any unnecessary purchases, you can revel in your success. However if there is a day when you bought something not within your plan do not look at it as a failure. Instead, view the purchase as a lapse and enjoy what you bought, knowing that tomorrow is another day. You will have another twenty-four hours to make choices that will either support or not support your plans to reach your goal. And if you find yourself consistently doing things that do not support your goals, review your goals, they may need to be adjusted. Viewing your goals in these terms gives you more chance of success.

Feeling fearful? Sometimes fear can show up as we start to change or as we challenge ourselves to do things different and better than before. Embrace the fear, it means you are moving and growing. Work through the fear, the best ways to do this are to write about your feelings in a journal, join a support group, talk to a trusted friend or a qualified professional. Fear is normal and as long as you do not let it control you is it okay. So step outside your comfort zone and work toward your dream!

And keep this in mind. Thinking about your goals is not enough to reach them. You have to write them down, plan and accomplish them. Along the way you will encounter challenges, your goals may change and you will add new ones. But that is all part of life and getting what you want.

"Unless you try to do something beyond what you have already mastered, you will never grow." Author Unknown.

"A ship in the harbor is safe...but that's not what ships were made for." Author Unknown

"When you have a dream, you've got to grab it and never let go." Carol Burnett

Revise Your List Often
Remember that your goals and dreams will change throughout the year. Review your list often. See if you're on track and make any changes you need to, resolution making, dreaming and goal setting are not something just done once a year on January 31st.

Make your goals and dreams more real. Say you dream of writing a great American novel. Photocopy a book cover and write your name in as the author. Look at this paper often. This trick makes far-reaching goals feel more attainable.

What *do* you want? A better job, more money, or to lose weight? How much? Be specific. Repeat your goal to yourself often. Place it on a card where you'll see a lot.

"Being challenged in life is inevitable. Being defeated is optional." Roger Crawford

I once worked with a client who had a life she enjoyed very much. The only thing she longed for was a loving partner to share her life with. We spoke at length about what she was doing to attract the right partner into her life. She explained that on occasion she would go to bars and nightclubs with friends in the hopes of meeting someone. When I asked her how that was going she said not too well. I asked her what else she was doing. She told me she allowed herself to be set up on blind dates by friends and family members. But she said that was not going very well either. I told her that it made sense to me that she had not found the right person yet. And this is why: She had not clearly defined what she wanted in a partner. Knowing she wanted to meet a man was not enough. In order to get what she wanted, she needed to know what she wanted.

So we did an exercise. I asked questions and together we complied a list of her ideal mate. Her ideal mate did not drink or smoke, no wonder she was having trouble meeting him in a bar. Her list took up two notebook pages and it got very specific. She listed physical characteristics like hair and eye color. She wrote about his family situation, she was an only child and had always wished for a large family. Things like attitude, physical appearance, career, future goals and hobbies made the list as well. One hobby she listed was reading because she was an avid reader and wanted to be able to discuss books.

I directed her to read her list at least once a week and to go places where her ideal mate might go. I asked her not to put

197

any pressure on herself and I explained that now that she had clearly defined what she wanted it would appear. We continued to meet weekly and she kept me updated on how things were going. She had been spending more time at a local chain bookstore researching a project she had been working on. There she had struck up a friendship with one of the workers. They talked at length whenever she was at the store and they even met for coffee one of his night's off. He invited her check out a book group he ran monthly there at the store. Two and a half months later they went on an official date. She e-mailed me as soon as she got home from the date. It turns out they had an unbelievable time! The more they spoke the more he seemed to be the type of guy she had been searching for. While we were on the phone she pulled out her list and we reviewed it. Turns out he was almost an exact match to the items she had listed.

Today they are married with two children and run a town bookstore together. She has shared her list with him and they both agree that defining what you want is the first and most important step to getting what you want.

Chapter Highlights
- Have specific goals in writing.
- Take steps toward achieving them.
- Read goals often.
- Revise goals as needed.

Chapter Resources
- successories.com - Motivational art, unique teambuilding tools, personalized awards, instant recognition and an exclusive selection of business gifts. 800-535-2773
- coachfederation.org - Professional coaches provide an ongoing partnership designed to help clients produce fulfilling results in their personal and professional lives. 888-423-3131

- Life U Love – 1-866-294-9900
  369 Evergreen Blvd.
  Scotch Plains, NJ 07076
  www.lifeulove.com – jamie@lifeulove.com

After that, do everything but move into a log cabin with no running water. AKA Simplifying and Getting Down to the Basics

This section is for you if you answer "yes" to any of the following:

- ➤ You have things in your house that you don't use or don't find attractive.
- ➤ You worry about things that never happen.
- ➤ You have trouble making up your mind.
- ➤ You have trouble accepting that you're not perfect.
- ➤ You overbook yourself.
- ➤ You wear your hair in such a way that it requires more than ten minutes to style.
- ➤ You tell little white lies.
- ➤ You have a large circle of friends and acquaintances.
- ➤ Your life feels complicated and difficult.

"Your life is too complicated when you've got a ringing phone in one hand, a double cappuccino in the other, and you need to make a left-hand turn." Elaine St. James

Introduction

A chapter on simplicity? I know I know, you're thinking I'm going to ask you to sell all your earthly possessions and move into a log cabin with no running water or electricity, right? Well, not exactly. We want simplified, not necessarily frugal.

What's Important to You?

The first thing to do is to take some time to define your priorities. What do I mean by this? I mean think long and hard about what's important to you at this point in your life. Or in other words, what do you want to be spending the majority of your time and energy on? Note that your priorities will change. You can always make adjustments to have your life reflect your current priorities.

So what are they? Finishing school? Spending more time with your family? Getting reacquainted with your spouse? Advancing your career? Whatever your priorities are, define and clarify them. Then you can begin to make choices about how you'll spend your time based on these priorities.

For example, if you list "spend time with my family" and you're asked to participate in a school bake sale, you might consider offering a small donation in lieu of your time and service. This accomplishes the school's goal of raising money while leaving your time free to spend with your family.

It's helpful to have your top three to five priorities written on an index card you can keep handy and read often. You can clip it to your calendar or tack it up by your phone. Additionally, once you have your priorities sorted out, you can actually schedule time to honor them. For example, maybe you listed "get reacquainted with my spouse." If so, then scheduling a date night might be a good idea. Choose a night that works for the both of you. Hire a babysitter so you can go out or have the kids visit either family or friends so you have the house to yourselves. I know two married couples who have rotating date nights. One couple watches the kids while the other goes out and then they switch the next week. It's inexpensive because they don't have to pay a babysitter. It is very important that you block the time out on your calendar to do the things that are important to you before all your time is taken up by other activities.

Stop often to and ask yourself how important is it? And be honest. When a friend calls and invites you to a Tupperware party, stop to consider how important it is. Depending on your answer, either accept or decline the offer. If you choose to decline, you can do so gracefully by offering to review the catalogue to possibly place an order.

Put a Post-it note on your calendar or by your phone that reads; how important is it?

You Have a Choice
Then there's the idea of making deliberate and thoughtful decisions. Sometimes we can get caught up in the hustle and bustle of our daily lives and we can forget we actually have a choice about each and every action we take. Although it may not feel like it, you do have a choice about how you spend your time.

Slow Down!
Stop and make decisions about your commitments based on how high activities rank on your list of priorities. And since we're talking about slowing down, actually do it. Eat slower. Drive slower. Talk slower. Do everything a little bit slower. This gives you time to digest and savors life's moments instead of seeing them flash by at record speed.

Imagine a slow, calm drive to work. You can stop to let a car go ahead of you and you are not grasping the steering wheel in a death grip. You can avoid stressing over why the cars in front of you can't go faster so you can make the light. Imagine giving yourself the time to arrive to work a little early. Not worrying that you'll be five or even ten minutes late. What a much more relaxing way to start your day!

When you slow down, you're more in tune with the moment, more aware of the present. And that's when you can begin to recognize that the present is perfect. You're right where you are supposed to be at this moment in time. Right now it happens that you are supposed to be reading this book! There are lessons to learn and moments to capture. All you have to know is that the present is indeed perfect. It does not get much simpler than that.

 Keep in mind that stopping is an option.

A Few Key Concepts
There are a few other key ideas to consider when you're in the process of streamlining your life; these include expecting nothing and being grateful for everything. The idea of expecting nothing and being grateful is powerful. Imagine never being disappointed and always being happy with whatever you get. This is a big idea to grasp. Even if you only manage to get a finger on it, your life will instantly become more pleasurable.

Also, look at how much you worry. I once saw a sign that read, worrying is mediating on the wrong stuff. How true is that? Often what we worry about never comes to be. And two, control your worry, it only expends your valuable energy. Walk through this little exercise whenever you find yourself worrying about something. Ask yourself, "Is this an issue I can do something about?" If the answer is yes, then do it. If the answer is no, then stop worrying.

Journaling also helps to control worry, you can write about what's concerning you.

Simple Ideas to Simplify Your Life

> ➤ Focus on what you have rather than what others have.
> ➤ Learn to be content with what you have today.
> ➤ Accept that you're not perfect.
> ➤ Don't overbook yourself.
> ➤ Tomorrow is another day with another chance.
> ➤ Wear an easy-to-care for hairstyle.
> ➤ Stick to the truth. Telling lies -- even little white ones – gets complicated.
> ➤ Keep a few, good, close friends.
> ➤ Work on being in the moment.
> ➤ When faced with what seems like a big decision, put it in perspective. Will your decision matter in three years? If not, make a choice and move on. You can always change your mind later on.

Make your life as easy and comfortable as possible. With the exception of difficult times, your life should be relatively easy. When making decisions about things that will affect your every day, think about your comfort. For example, when purchasing a bed, don't just purchase the one on sale. This is something that you'll use every day and have for a long time. Pick something that you absolutely love, even if it costs a little more.

Be yourself. If you have straight hair, find a flattering hairstyle for straight hair instead of getting a perm. Don't use color; it requires high maintenance. Wear little or no makeup. Use clear nail polish or a light color; it does not show chips as quickly.

Take Responsibility

Be accountable and take responsibility for your words and actions. It has become commonplace to pass the blame, to insist it must be someone else's fault. You have probably heard the story about the woman who got a cup of coffee, burned herself, and sued the restaurant company that gave her the coffee. There's a feeling of that's okay, it's not your fault, sue the other person. Well it's your fault if you get burned. Live with the consequences and learn from them. It makes your life much simpler.

I once worked with a client who had an overwhelming amount of stuff to do. She was never done with her "to do" list. We looked at what was making all this extra work for her, and we found it was little things that could be changed. For example, she had many live plants all throughout her house. They needed constant care from watering, to pruning, to repotting and fertilizing. She made one seemingly small change and it had far reaching effects. She gave away all her live plants and replaced them with a nice selection of silk plants. They were just as attractive, yet they required no care. Ask yourself, what is making extra work for me?

Make Your List

Lastly, when you think about streamlining your life you'll find there are a lot of areas that can be adjusted. Simplifying your thoughts, your possessions, your environment and much more. Sit down soon in one of your favorite spots at home with pen and paper in hand and make your list.

One area of simplifying that's often overlooked is noise. See what noise can be eliminated or at least decreased in you life. These noises -- no matter how small and how much you think you can tune it out -- distracts us and complicates our world.

If I Had My Life to Live Over Again
by Erma Bombeck

Erma Bombeck wrote this article, after she found out that she had breast cancer. Bombeck had a mastectomy shortly thereafter-in 1991. She died five years later.

- ➢ I would have gone to bed when I was sick instead of pretending the earth would go into a holding pattern if I weren't there for the day.

- ➢ I would have burned the pink candle sculpted like a rose before it melted in storage.

- ➢ I would have talked less and listened more.

- ➢ I would have invited friends over to dinner even if the carpet was stained, or the sofa faded.

- ➢ I would have eaten the popcorn in the "good" living room and worried much less about the dirt when someone wanted to light a fire in the fireplace.

- ➢ I would have taken the time to listen to my Grandfather ramble about his youth.

- ➢ I would never have insisted the car windows be rolled up on a summer day because my hair had just been teased and sprayed.

- ➢ I would have sat on the lawn with my children and not worried about grass stains.

- ➢ I would have cried and laughed less while watching television and more while watching life.

- ➤ I would never have bought anything just because it was practical, wouldn't show soil, or was guaranteed to last a lifetime.

- ➤ Instead of wishing away nine months of pregnancy, I'd have cherished every moment and realized that the wonderment growing inside me was the only chance in life to assist God in a miracle.

- ➤ When my kids kissed me impetuously I would never have said, "Later. Now go get washed up for dinner."

- ➤ There would have been more "I love you's." More "I'm sorry's"...

- ➤ But mostly, given another shot at life, I would seize every minute...look at it and really see it...live it...and never give it back.

- ➤ Stop sweating the small stuff. Don't worry about who doesn't like you, who has more, or who's doing what.

Imagine that you were just told you only had a short time to live. What would you change? Don't wait; change it today!

And remember the words of Erma. How will you look back on your life? With thoughts of regret, wishes and should have's or thoughts full of wonderful memories of happy times, having done what you wanted, having shared, laughed and loved.

Low maintenance. By making this phrase your new mantra or affirmation, you'll make choices that will make your life easier, simpler and more streamlined.

Chapter Highlights
- Define and stick to your priorities.
- Start asking yourself, "How important is it?"
- Slow down.
- Remember that stopping is an option.
- Be accountable for your actions and words.

Chapter Resources
- I Could Do Anything if I Only Knew What It Was: How to Discover What You Really Want and How to Get It - Barbara Sher
- Complete Idiot's Guide to Reaching Your Goals, Jeff P. Davidson
- Life U Love
  369 Evergreen Blvd.
  Scotch Plains, NJ 07076
  866-294-9900
  www.lifeulove.com - jamie@lifeulove.com

Now tie it up in a nice, neat package.
AKA Pulling It All Together

These nine steps give you a wealth of information you can use to make changes to start creating a life you love. To avoid becoming overwhelmed, it's important to give yourself time. It takes twenty-eight days to create a new habit. And there should be time for evaluating the new ways of doing things. Find out what's working and what's not.

I always love to hear from readers about how their lives have changed. Please contact me with your story; it may be used in an upcoming book. Send your letter to: Jamie Novak, Life U Love, 369 Evergreen Blvd., Scotch Plains, NJ 07076 or e-mail <u>Jamie@LifeULove.com</u>.

Chapter Resources
- http://www.simpleliving.com A wonderful site for some insight into living simply. You can also subscribe for a free e-mail newsletter.
- The Simplicity Reader: Simplify Your Life; Inner Simplicity; Living the Simple Life
- Living the Simple Life: A Guide to Scaling Down & Enjoying More

- Simplify Your Life: Slow Down and Enjoy the Things That Really Matter
- Inner Simplicity: 100 Ways to Regain Peace and Nourish Your Soul
- Simplify Your Life with Kids: 100 Ways to Make Family Life Easier and More Fun

All written by Elaine St. James

- Life U Love
  369 Evergreen Blvd.
  Scotch Plains, NJ 07076
  866-294-9900
  www.lifeulove.com
  jamie@lifeulove.com

APPENDIX

Retention Schedule

Here's a retention schedule to help you choose what to keep and what to toss:

- Adoption records - forever (safety deposit or fire proof container)

- Annual investment papers - 3 years

- Appraisals - forever

- ATM receipts - 1 month; balance checkbook, then toss.

- Bank statements - 3 years for tax

- Bills (paid, deductible) - 7 year

- Bills (paid, non-deductible) - 1 year

- Bills of sale - forever

- Birth certificate(s) – forever (safety deposit or fire proof container)

- Canceled checks - deductible - 7 years for taxes

- Canceled checks - non-deductible - 3 years for taxes

- Canceled insurance policies - 3 years

- Car maintenance – while you have the car

- Car title - while you have the car

- College transcript – forever

- Contracts - while active

- Credit card receipts and statements - 3 years for taxes

- Death certificates – forever (safety deposit or fire proof container)

- Deed - forever

- Diploma - forever

- Divorce decree – forever

- Documents and receipts to support income or deduction - 3 years

- Frequent flyer program information - Keep only the most recent statement.

- Home improvement records – while active

- Income tax returns with cancelled check or refund check stub - 7 years

- Insurance policies – while active

- Certificate of deposit - 1 year

- Investment statements - Keep only the year end; 7 years.

- Living will - forever (safety deposit or fire proof container)

- Loan statements - 7 years

- Medical/dental bills - 3 years

- Money market - Keep only the most recent.

- Mortgage records (paid) – forever (safety deposit or fire proof container)

- Marriage license - forever (safety deposit or fire proof)

- Pay stubs - 3 years

- Pensions – while active

- Property records – while active

- Property tax records - while active

- Quarterly investment statement – Toss quarterly once you get the yearly; Keep yearly for 3 years.

- Real estate closing documents – forever

- Retirement plans – while active

- Stock certificates – while active

- Stock receipts – 3 years

- Stock records – while active

- Tax bills - while active

- Utility bills - 3 years

- Will - forever (safety deposit or fire proof container)

Master Packing List
(for vacation and business travel)

Clothing (Men)

Clothing/Accessories:
- ❑ Belt
- ❑ Coat
- ❑ Dress pants
- ❑ Dress shirts
- ❑ Shoes
- ❑ Socks
- ❑ Sleepwear
- ❑ Bathrobe
- ❑ Slippers
- ❑ Sports coat
- ❑ Cufflinks/studs
- ❑ Suit
- ❑ Tie
- ❑ Tie tack/clip
- ❑ Undershirts
- ❑ Underwear
- ❑ Watch

Casual Wear/Workout Wear:
- ❑ Casual outfit
- ❑ Flip-flops
- ❑ Jeans
- ❑ Shorts
- ❑ Sneakers
- ❑ Socks
- ❑ Sports equipment
- ❑ Swim goggles
- ❑ Swimsuit
- ❑ Workout wear

Weather Wear:
- ❑ Boots
- ❑ Coat
- ❑ Earmuffs
- ❑ Gloves
- ❑ Hat
- ❑ Sandals
- ❑ Scarf
- ❑ Umbrella

Clothing (Women)

Clothing/Accessories:
- ❑ Bathrobe
- ❑ Belt
- ❑ Bra
- ❑ Coat
- ❑ Dress pants
- ❑ Dress shirts
- ❑ Dresses
- ❑ Earrings
- ❑ Necklace
- ❑ Nylons
- ❑ Pins
- ❑ Rings
- ❑ Scarves
- ❑ Shoes
- ❑ Skirts
- ❑ Sleepwear
- ❑ Slip
- ❑ Slippers
- ❑ Socks
- ❑ Suit
- ❑ Sweater
- ❑ Underwear
- ❑ Watch

Casual Wear/Workout Wear:
- ❑ Casual outfit
- ❑ Cover-up
- ❑ Flip-flops
- ❑ Jeans
- ❑ Shorts
- ❑ Sneakers
- ❑ Socks

Clothing (Women) (cont'd.)

Casual Wear/Workout Wear:
- [ ] Sports Equipment
- [ ] Swim Goggles
- [ ] Swimsuit
- [ ] Workout wear

Weather Wear:
- [ ] Boots
- [ ] Coat
- [ ] Earmuffs
- [ ] Gloves
- [ ] Hat
- [ ] Sandals
- [ ] Scarf
- [ ] Umbrella

Electronics:
- [ ] AC charger cord
- [ ] Batteries
- [ ] Camera
- [ ] CD cassette player
- [ ] Cell phone
- [ ] Cell phone charger cords
- [ ] Computer
- [ ] Cords & plugs
- [ ] Digital camera
- [ ] Film
- [ ] Mini tape recorder
- [ ] Pager
- [ ] Palm pilot
- [ ] Travel alarm

Work Stuff/Traveling Information:
- [ ] Airport shuttle information
- [ ] Briefcase
- [ ] Business cards
- [ ] Cash
- [ ] Client information
- [ ] Company letterhead and stationery
- [ ] Coupons for destination city
- [ ] Credit cards
- [ ] Demo material
- [ ] Directions
- [ ] Emergency telephone numbers
- [ ] Envelopes for receipts
- [ ] Flight tickets
- [ ] Guidebooks
- [ ] Identification (including a photo)
- [ ] Maps
- [ ] Organizer
- [ ] Overhead transparencies
- [ ] Paperwork
- [ ] Pen
- [ ] Pointer
- [ ] Postage
- [ ] Preprinted labels for those you plan to write
- [ ] Presentation material
- [ ] Promo material
- [ ] Reading material
- [ ] Rental car information
- [ ] Slides
- [ ] Sunglasses
- [ ] Travel journal
- [ ] Travelers' checks
- [ ] VIP/frequent flyer pass
- [ ] White board pens
- [ ] Writing pad

Medicine Cabinet/Toiletries:

- ❏ Aftershave
- ❏ Allergy medicine
- ❏ Antacid
- ❏ Antibacterial cream
- ❏ Asthma medication
- ❏ Athletes foot spray
- ❏ Band-aids
- ❏ Birth control
- ❏ Blow dryer
- ❏ Brush
- ❏ Chapstick
- ❏ Cologne
- ❏ Comb
- ❏ Conditioner
- ❏ Contact lens
- ❏ Contact lens solution
- ❏ Cotton balls
- ❏ Cream/Lotion (body, hand, eye and face)
- ❏ Curling iron
- Dental floss
- ❏ Diarrhea medicine
- ❏ Dramamine
- ❏ Earplugs
- ❏ Emergency sewing kit
- ❏ Extra razor blades
- ❏ Eye drops
- ❏ Facial cleaner
- ❏ Feminine protection
- ❏ Gel
- ❏ Hair accessories
- ❏ Hairspray
- ❏ Headache medication
- ❏ Makeup
- ❏ Makeup remover
- ❏ Mosquito repellant
- ❏ Mousse
- ❏ Mouthwash
- ❏ Nail clippers
- ❏ Nail file
- ❏ Nail polish
- ❏ Nail polish remover
- ❏ Perfume
- ❏ Prescription glasses
- ❏ Prescription medications
- ❏ Q-tips
- ❏ Razor
- ❏ Safety pins
- ❏ Shampoo
- ❏ Shaving cream
- ❏ Shoe polish
- ❏ Soap
- ❏ Sunscreen
- ❏ Toothbrush
- ❏ Toothpaste
- ❏ Topical ointments
- ❏ Tweezers
- ❏ Vitamins

Miscellaneous:

- ❏ Coffee/tea/sweetener
- ❏ Entertainment
- ❏ Extra duffle bag for souvenirs
- ❏ Flashlight
- ❏ Games
- ❏ Gum
- ❏ Iron/steamer
- ❏ Laundry bag
- ❏ Pillow
- ❏ Snacks/energy bars
- ❏ Stationery/thank you notes
- ❏ Tote bag/backpack

International travel:

- ❑ Electric adaptor kit (110V adaptor)
- ❑ Electronic translator
- ❑ Foreign language book/dictionary
- ❑ Medication for tropical diseases
- ❑ Passport/Visa

Slow Cooker Recipes

Pot Roast	
4 medium potatoes, cubed 4 carrots, sliced 1 onion, sliced 3-4 lbs. Rump roast, cut into serving size pieces 1 tsp. Salt ½ tsp. Pepper 1 bouillon cube ½ C boiling water	Put vegetables and meat in the slow cooker. Stir in the salt and pepper. Dissolve the bouillon cube in the boiling water and pour over the other ingredients. Cover and cook on low for 10-12 hours. Serves 8.

Beef Stroganoff	
2 Tbs.. flour ½ tsp. garlic powder ½ tsp. Pepper ¼ tsp. Paprika 1 ¾ lbs. Boneless beef round steak 10 ¾ oz. Cream of mushroom soup ½ C water 1 envelope dried onion soup mix 9 oz. Jar sliced mushrooms, drained ½ C sour cream 1 Tbs.. minced fresh parsley	Combine flour, garlic powder, pepper and paprika in slow cooker. Cut meat into 1 ½ " x ½" strips. Place meat in flour mixture and toss until coated. Add mushroom soup, water and soup mix; stir until well mixed. Cover the slow cooker, and cook on high 3-3 ½ hours or on low 6-7 hours. Stir in sour cream and parsley. Cover and cook on high 10-15 minutes. Can be served over egg noodles. Serves 6.

Italian Pork Chop	
16 oz. Italian salad dressing 4 pork chops 2 potatoes, cubed 2 carrots, sliced 1 medium onion, sliced	Place pork chops in the slow cooker. Add in potatoes, carrots and onion. Pour salad dressing over them and cover. Cook on high 6-8- hours. Serves 4.

BBQ Ribs	
3-4 baby back or spare ribs ½ tsp. Salt ½ tsp. Pepper 2 onions, sliced 16 oz. BBQ sauce	Brown the ribs under a broiler. Slice into serving size pieces. Season and place in slow cooker. Add onions and BBQ sauce. Cover and cook on low for 6 hours. Serves 4-6.

Spaghetti with meat sauce	
1 lb. Ground beef 2 28 oz. Cans of tomatoes 2 medium onions, quartered 2 medium carrots, cut into chunks 2 garlic cloves, minced 6 oz. Tomato paste 2 Tbs.. Chopped fresh parsley 1 bay leaf 1 Tbs.. Sugar 1 tsp. Dried basil ¾ tsp. Salt ½ tsp. Dried oregano Dash of pepper 2 Tbs.. cold water 2 Tbs.. cornstarch Hot cooked spaghetti Grated Parmesan cheese	Place meat in the slow cooker. In a blender, combine 1 can of tomatoes plus the onion, carrots and garlic. Blend until finely chopped and stir into meat. Cut up remaining tomatoes and stir into meat mix. Add tomato paste, parsley, bay leaf, sugar, basil, salt, oregano and pepper; mix well. Cover and cook 8-10 hours on low. Before serving, turn to high, remove bay leaf, cover and heat until bubbly (about 10 minutes). Combine water and cornstarch; stir into tomato mix. Cook another 10 minutes, then serve sauce with spaghetti and parmesan cheese. Serves 8-10.

Mushroom Chicken	
6 boneless skinless frozen chicken breast cut in halves 2 10 ¾ oz. cans of cream of chicken or cream of mushroom soup 4 oz. can sliced mushrooms or ½ C fresh mushrooms sliced ¾ tsp. Salt 1/3 tsp. Pepper	Place frozen chicken in slow cooker. Mix together soup, mushrooms, salt and pepper; pour over chicken and cover. Cook 10-12 hours on low. Serves 6.

Chicken Teriyaki	
2-3 lbs. skinless chicken pieces 20 oz. can of pineapple chunks Dash of ground ginger 1 C teriyaki sauce	Place chicken in slow cooker. Pour remaining ingredients over chicken. Cook low 6-8 hours or high 4-6 hours. Serves 6.

Chocolate Pudding Cake	
18 ½ oz. package chocolate cake mix 3.9 oz. package instant chocolate pudding mix 2 C sour cream 4 eggs 1 C water ¾ C oil 1 C semi-sweet chocolate chips	Combine cake mix, pudding mix, sour cream, eggs, water and oil in electric mixer bowl. Beat on medium speed for 2 minutes and then stir in chocolate chips. Pour into a greased slow cooker, cover and cook 6-7 hours low or 3-4 hours high or until tooth pick is inserted and comes out clean. Serves 10-12.

Lasagna	
8 lasagna noodles uncooked 1 lb. ground beef 1 tsp. Italian seasoning 28 oz. jar spaghetti sauce 1/3 C water 4 oz. can sliced mushrooms 15 oz. ricotta cheese 2 C shredded mozzarella cheese	Break noodles. Place ½ in the bottom of a greased slow cooker. Brown the ground beef in a saucepan drain and stir in the Italian seasoning. Spread half of the ground beef over the noodles. Layer half the sauce and water, half the mushrooms, half the ricotta, half the mozzarella over the beef and then repeat the layers. Cover and cook on low for 5 hours. Serves 8.

Chili con Queso	
20 oz. can refried beans 1 C shredded cheddar ½ C chopped green onions ¼ tsp. Salt 2-4 Tbs. bottled taco sauce Tortilla chips	Combine beans, cheese, onions, salt, and taco sauce in slow cooker. Cover and cook low 2-2 ½ hours or high 30 minutes and then low 30 minutes. Serve with chips. Serves 6.

Egg and Cheese Bake	
3 C toasted bread cubes 1 ½ C shredded cheddar cheese Fried crumbled bacon or ham chunks 6 eggs beaten 3 C milk ¾ tsp. salt ¼ tsp. pepper	Combine bread cubes, cheese and meat in greased slow cooker. Mix together the eggs, milk, salt and pepper. Pour over bread cubes, cheese and meat in slow cooker. Cook on low 4-6 hours Serves 6.

Veggie Soup	
1 lb. round steak, cut into ½" pieces 14 ½ oz. can diced tomatoes 3 C water 2 potatoes, peeled and cubed 2 onions, sliced 3 celery stalks, sliced 2 carrots, sliced 3 beef bouillon cubes ½ tsp. dried basil ½ tsp. dried oregano 1 tsp. salt ¼ tsp. pepper 1 ½ C frozen mixed vegetables	Combine steak, tomatoes, water and beef bouillon cubes in slow cooker. Cover and cook 6 hours. Add everything else and cook on high 2 hours until tender. Serves 10.

X

Minestrone	
1 lb. beef stewing meat 6 C water 28 oz. can of tomatoes diced and undrained 1 beef bouillon cube 1 medium onion, chopped 2 Tbs. minced diced parsley 1 ½ tsp. salt 1 ½ tsp. Dried thyme ½ tsp. pepper 1 medium zucchini, thinly sliced 2 C cabbage, finely chopped 16 oz. can garbanzo beans drained 1 C uncooked small elbow or shell macaroni ¼ C grated Parmesan cheese	Combine beef, water, tomatoes, bouillon, onion, parsley, salt, thyme and pepper. Cover and cook on low 7-9 hours until meat is tender. Stir in the zucchini, cabbage, beans, and macaroni. Cover and cook on high 30-45 minutes until vegetables are tender, then sprinkle with cheese and serve. Serves 8.

Lemon chicken	
1 apple peeled, cored and quartered 1 celery stalk, chopped 1 (3 lb.) chicken dash of salt dash of pepper 1 onion, chopped ½ tsp. Dried rosemary, crushed 1 lemon, juiced 1 C hot water	Place apple and celery in the chicken. Rub the skin with salt and pepper. Place chicken in the cooker. Sprinkle with onion, rosemary and lemon juice. Add hot water and cover. Cook low 6-8 hours. Serves 4.

Budget Worksheet

	Monthly Budget Amount	Monthly Actual Amount	Difference
Income			
Wages Paid			
Bonuses			
Interest Income			
Capital Gains Income			
Dividend Income			
Miscellaneous Income			
Income Subtotal			
Expenses			
Mortgage/Rent			
Utilities			
Gas			
Water			
Electric			
Sewer			
Garbage			
Cable TV			
Telephone			
Cell Phone			
Pager			
Home Repairs /Main			
Car Payment(s)			
Car Insurance			
Gas/Car Fuel			
Auto Repairs/ Maintenance/Fees			
Parking			
Other Trans (tolls, EZ Pass, subway etc)			
Childcare			
Home Owners/Renter Insurance			
Computer Expense (internet access)			
Entertainment/ Recreation			
Groceries			
Eating Out			
School Tuition			

	Monthly Budget Amount	Monthly Actual Amount	Difference
Cc Payments			
Other Monthly Payments w/ or w/o Interest			
Monthly Loan payments			
Extra Curricular Activities			
Dry Cleaning			
Housekeeper			
Gardner			
Gifts/Donations			
Healthcare (medical dental vision ins) and copays			
Prescriptions			
Hobbies/Kids Lessons			
Charity/Donations			
Interest Expenses (mortgage, cc fees)			
Newspaper/Magazine Subscriptions			
Memberships (health club, book club, music club)			
Federal Income Tax			
State Income Tax			
Social Security/Medicare Tax			
Property Tax			
Pets			
Misc. Expenses			
Xmas Club			
401K Cont			
Set Amount for Savings			
Expenses Subtotal			

Subtract the totals for the monthly expenses from the total monthly income? Is the balance more or less?

Multiply weekly payments by 4 or divide yearly payments by 12 to apply to the worksheet.

Carry a small notebook, jot down everything you spend. Carry an envelope for the receipts, cash purchase, whenever you make one, get a receipt, no matter how small.

Master Grocery Shopping List

Baked Goods		Canned Foods	
Baked Goods		**Canned Foods**	
☐	Bagels	☐	Beans
☐	Bread, white	☐	Corn
☐	Bread, wheat	☐	Cranberry Sauce
☐	Hard Rolls	☐	Fruit
☐	Muffins	☐	Mushrooms
☐	Other:	☐	Peas
Condiments		☐	Tomatoes
☐	Bacon Bits	☐	Tomato Sauce
☐	Barbecue Sauce	☐	Tuna
☐	Chocolate Syrup	**Soup**	
☐	Jelly	☐	Chicken noodle
☐	Ketchup	☐	Cream of celery
☐	Marshmallows	☐	Cream of chicken
☐	Mayonnaise		
☐	Mustard	☐	Cream of mushroom
☐	Non-Stick Spray		
☐	Olives, black	☐	Tomato Soup
☐	Olives, green	**Frozen Foods**	
☐	Peanut butter	☐	Cakes
☐	Pickles	☐	Chicken Nuggets/Filets
☐	Salad Dressing		
☐	Soy Sauce	☐	Dinners
☐	Steak Sauce	☐	Fish sticks
☐	Syrup	☐	French Toast
☐	Tartar Sauce	☐	French Fries
☐	Vinegar	☐	Ice Cream
☐		☐	Juice concentrates
☐			
☐		☐	Pancakes
☐		☐	Pies
Cereals		☐	Pizza
☐	Kids Cereal	☐	Pot Pies
☐	Adult Cereal	☐	Tater Tots
☐	Oatmeal	☐	Vegetables
☐	Other:	☐	Waffles
Cookies		**Dairy**	
☐	Chocolate Chip	☐	Butter
☐	Crackers	☐	American cheese
☐	Graham Crackers	☐	Cheddar cheese
☐	Other:	☐	Cottage cheese

	Dairy (cont'd.)		Drinks/Mixes
☐	Cream Cheese	☐	Apple juice
☐	Mozzarella Cheese	☐	Club soda
		☐	Fruit punch
☐	Dips	☐	Grapefruit juice
☐	Eggs	☐	Juice Boxes
☐	Half & Half	☐	Kool-Aid
☐	Jell-O	☐	Lemonade
☐	Margarine	☐	Orange juice
☐	Milk	☐	Powdered milk
☐	Chocolate milk	☐	Soda
☐	Pudding	☐	Seltzer
☐	Sour Cream	☐	Sports drink
☐	Tofu	☐	Tang
☐	Tortillas	☐	Water
☐	Yogurt	☐	
☐	Whipped cream	**Paper/Kitchen Products**	
☐			
☐		☐	Aluminum Foil
Hot Beverages		☐	Freezer bags
☐	Apple cider	☐	Heavy duty trash bags
☐	Cappuccino		
☐	Coffee	☐	Kitchen garbage bags
☐	Coffee creamer		
☐	Coffee filters	☐	Kleenex/Tissues
☐	Hot chocolate	☐	Lunch bags
☐	Tea	☐	Paper cups
☐	Tea bags	☐	Paper plates
☐		☐	Paper towels
☐		☐	Plastic sandwich bags
☐			
Deli		☐	Plastic wrap
☐	Bacon	☐	Plastic utensils
☐	Bologna	☐	Snack bags
☐	Ham	☐	Toilet paper
☐	Hot Dogs	☐	Waxed paper
☐	Pastrami	**Pet Supplies**	
☐	Roast Beef	☐	Bird seed
☐	Salami	☐	Canned cat food
☐	Sausage	☐	Canned dog food
☐	Turkey	☐	Cat litter
☐	Lunchables	☐	Dry cat food
☐	Sliced cheese	☐	Dry dog food
☐	Macaroni salad	☐	Pet treats
☐	Potato salad	☐	
☐	Roasted whole chicken	☐	
		☐	

	Pastas/Rice/Starches		
☐	Dinner helpers	☐	Celery
☐	Egg noodles	☐	Cauliflower
☐	Fettuccini	☐	Cherries
☐	Gravy	☐	Corn
☐	Instant potatoes	☐	Cucumber
☐	Lasagna	☐	Eggplant
☐	Linguine	☐	Figs
☐	Macaroni and cheese	☐	Grapefruit
		☐	Grapes
☐	Parmesan cheese	☐	Green peppers
☐	Spaghetti	☐	Green beans
☐	Spaghetti sauce	☐	Garlic
☐	Stuffing mix	☐	Honeydew melon
☐	Taco mix	☐	Kiwi
☐	Velveeta cheese	☐	Lettuce
☐	White rice	☐	Mango
☐	Wild rice	☐	Mushrooms
☐	Yellow rice	☐	Nectarines
☐	Ziti	☐	Onions
Seafood		☐	Oranges
☐	Clams	☐	Papaya
☐	Crabmeat	☐	Parsley
☐	Fish Filets/Steak	☐	Parsnips
☐	Lobster	☐	Peaches
☐	Oysters	☐	Pears
☐	Mussels	☐	Peas
☐	Salmon	☐	Pineapple
☐	Scallops	☐	Plums
☐	Shrimp	☐	Potatoes
☐	Tuna	☐	Radishes
Produce/Fruits		☐	Raisins
☐	Apples	☐	Red peppers
☐	Artichokes	☐	Scallions
☐	Apricots	☐	Shallots
☐	Asparagus	☐	Spinach
☐	Avocado	☐	Squash
☐	Beets	☐	Strawberries
☐	Bananas	☐	Tangerines
☐	Blueberries	☐	Tomatoes
☐	Broccoli	☐	Watermelon
☐	Brussels sprouts	☐	Yams
☐	Cabbage	☐	Zucchini
☐	Cantaloupe	☐	
☐	Carrots	☐	

Spices/Baking Products		Meat (cont'd.)	
☐	Baking powder	☐	Steaks
☐	Baking soda	☐	Veal
☐	Brown sugar	☐	
☐	Cake mix	☐	
☐	Cornstarch	☐	
☐	Flour	☐	
☐	Food coloring	☐	
☐	Garlic powder	**Snacks**	
☐	Icing	☐	Candy
☐	Italian seasoning	☐	Cereal Bars
☐	Jell-O mix	☐	Crackers
☐	Parsley flakes	☐	Gum
☐	Paprika	☐	Fruit Roll Ups
☐	Pepper	☐	Peanuts
☐	Pie shells	☐	Popcorn
☐	Powdered sugar	☐	Potato Chips
☐	Pudding mix	☐	
☐	Oregano	**Household**	
☐	Sugar sub	☐	All purpose cleaner
☐	Shortening		
☐	Vanilla flavoring	☐	Air freshener
☐	White sugar	☐	Batteries
☐	Yeast	☐	Bleach
☐		☐	Candles
Meat		☐	Carpet deodorizer
☐	Beef	☐	Car wash materials
☐	Bacon		
☐	Chicken	☐	Charcoal
☐	Ground beef	☐	Disinfectant
☐	Ground turkey	☐	Dishwashing liquid
☐	Ham		
☐	Lamb	☐	Dishwasher detergent
☐	Liver		
☐	Pork	☐	Drain cleaner
☐	Ribs	☐	Fabric softener
☐	Sausage	☐	Floor wax

Household (cont'd.)		Health and Beauty Items (cont'd.)	
☐	Film	☐	Laxatives
☐	Furniture polish	☐	Lip balm
☐	Glass cleaner	☐	Mouthwash
☐	Insect spray	☐	Pepto Bismal
☐	Laundry detergent	☐	Powder
		☐	Toothpaste
☐	Lightbulbs	☐	
☐	Matches	**Baby Products**	
☐	Oven cleaner	☐	Baby food
☐	Scouring pads	☐	Baby lotion
☐	Sponges	☐	Baby powder
☐	Stain remover	☐	Baby wash
☐	Tapes (video/ cassettes)	☐	Baby wipes
		☐	Baby shampoo
☐	Toilet bowl cleaner	☐	Diaper rash ointment
☐	Water filter	☐	Diapers
Health and Beauty Items		**Stationery**	
		☐	3-ring notebook
☐	Adhesive tape	☐	Crayons
☐	Anti-acid/ anti-gas	☐	Envelopes
		☐	Glue
☐	Antibiotic ointment	☐	Laundry Marker
		☐	Loose-leaf paper
☐	Antihistamine aspirin		Markers
		☐	Notepads
☐	Bandages	☐	Pencils
☐	Cold medicine	☐	Pens
☐	Contacts supplies	☐	Permanent marker
☐	Cotton balls		
☐	Cotton swabs	**Miscellaneous**	
☐	Cough syrup	☐	
☐	Dental floss	☐	
☐	Deodorant	☐	
☐	Eye drops	☐	
☐	First aid cream	☐	
☐	Hair conditioner	☐	
☐	Hair color	☐	
☐	Hair gel	☐	
☐	Hair mousse	☐	
☐	Hair spray	☐	
☐	Hand soap	☐	

"TO DO" LIST

THINGS TO DO TODAY
Day: _____

Appointments and telephone calls

_____	_____
_____	_____
_____	_____
_____	_____
_____	_____

Check when completed

1. _____ ❏

2. _____ ❏

3. _____ ❏

4. _____ ❏

5. _____ ❏

6. _____ ❏

7. _____ ❏

8. _____ ❏

9. _____ ❏

10. _____ ❏

Journaling Prompts

If you are finding it difficult to get started with journaling, here are some prompts to help you on your way.

Try to use all five senses when you write. Don't forget to describe how things look and smell and feel to the touch.

Start with today's date and the day of the week.

Then describe:

> ➤ The weather
> ➤ What you wore
> ➤ What you did
> ➤ Who you saw

You can also include:

> ➤ Major news events of the day
> ➤ What you are currently reading or watching on television
> ➤ What you ate
> ➤ The best part of the day and the worst part of the day

Here are some questions that may be interesting to answer:

> ➤ What is your earliest memory?
> ➤ As a child, who were your friends and what did you play?
> ➤ How did you get to school and what do you remember seeing on the way?
> ➤ As a child, what were you responsible for?

- ➢ As a child, what could you spend hours doing?

- ➢ What were some of your favorite games as a child?

- ➢ What were some of your family traditions?

- ➢ What do you remember most about the holidays?

- ➢ What was/is your favorite outfit?

- ➢ What is your favorite season and why?

- ➢ What is outside your window.

I remember…

- ➢ What is your earliest memory?

- ➢ Write about a place you've visited or would like to see.

Other, quirkier questions to ask yourself are:

- ➢ If you could be a song what song would you be and why?
- ➢ A movie
- ➢ A spice
- ➢ A book
- ➢ A color
- ➢ A tree
- ➢ A flower
- ➢ A food
- ➢ A drink
- ➢ A flavor
- ➢ A fish
- ➢ A season
- ➢ A shape
- ➢ A noise
- ➢ A time of day

Stain Buster Chart

To force the stain out of a fabric not soaked through it, try the following. Apply stain removers and solutions to the underside of the stain with the soiled area face down on a clean paper towel.

Fabric Stains

Stain	Treatment
Ballpoint Ink	Press a paper towel against the stain to absorb the wet ink. Using a cotton swab dipped in rubbing alcohol, lightly dab the mark. Rinse with cold water, then wash. Alternate to rubbing alcohol, spritz stain with hair spray.
Blood	Soak the stained garment for fifteen minutes in a bucket of cold water mixed with a handful of salt. Then soak in detergent and wash.
Chocolate	Pretreat stain with detergent, then wash.
Coffee (black or with sugar)	Flush with cool water, then rub the stain with a paste of powdered detergent and water, wash.
Coffee (with cream)	Flush with cool water, then sponge stain with a dry cleaning solvent. Allow to air dry, then rub the area with detergent. Wash.
Dirt/mud	Allow mud to dry. Brush off any hard residue, then wash. For deep stains, sponge with rubbing alcohol.
Fruit Juice	Rinse immediately under cold water. Treat any remaining stain by sponging it with rubbing alcohol. Wash.
Grass	Soak in detergent and wash.

Stain	Treatment
Grease, Oil, Fat	With a paper towel, blot away any remaining grease. Sponge with dry cleaning solution. Wash.
Lipstick	Dilute by sponging stain with rubbing alcohol. Repeat with dishwashing liquid. Wash.
Liquid Medicine, Cough Syrup	Sponge stain lightly with rubbing alcohol. Wash.
Mildew	Brush off mildewed area, pretreat area with a liquid detergent. Wash in the hottest water safe for that fabric, and dry in the sun.
Paint (latex)	Blot excess paint immediately, then sponge with cold water. Wash.
Pencil	Rub with art gum eraser
Perspiration	Pretreat stains by blotting ammonia solution (1 tsp. ammonia to 2 C water.) Wash.
Sauces (tomato based)	Place the fresh stain under cold water and rub between your fingers. Saturate the area with a pre-wash treatment and wash.
Wax	Scrape as much as you can off using a spoon. Place a brown bag over the spot, and iron on a warm setting until the wax melts into the paper. Treat any remaining stain with rubbing alcohol and then wash.
Wine (red)	Blot dry, then rinse fresh stains in cold water. Pretreat with a paste of powdered detergent and water, then wash in the hottest water safe for that fabric.

Stain	Treatment
Wine (white)	Flush with cold water and dab any spot that remains with dishwashing liquid. Wash.

Wallpaper

Stain	Treatment
Crayon	Make a paste with baking soda and mineral spirits. Use a cloth and rub away marks.
Felt Tip Marker	Apply rubbing alcohol and blot with paper towels.
Fingerprints, Smudges	Rub the area with an art gum eraser.
Grease	Hold several white paper towels over the spot and press with a lukewarm iron until the grease is absorbed. Follow by sponging the area with diluted dish liquid.

Carpets

Stain	Treatment
Alcoholic beverages	Apply detergent solution (1/4 tsp. clear non-bleach dishwashing liquid to 1 C warm water.) Allow to sit 10 minutes. Rinse with warm water and blot. If stain remains, follow with an ammonia solution (2 Tbs. colorless ammonia to 1 C lukewarm water.) Blot until dry.
Chewing Gum	Place ice cubes on the chewing gum. Wait ten minutes. Once the gum is hard, scrape it off.
Pet Accidents	Wet with vinegar solution (1 part white vinegar to 1 part lukewarm water) and apply to spot. Blot dry and repeat if necessary.

Stain	Treatment
Soft Drinks	Blot with paper towel until dry. With a clean cloth, apply water/detergent mixture (1 C warm water to 1 tsp. mild hand washing detergent.) If stain remains, blot with a water/vinegar solution of 1 C water to 2 Tbs. distilled white vinegar.) Use a clean towel to blot.

Try, try again. It may take more than one time to get the full effect of the treatment.

Work from the outside edges to the center. This prevents the spill from spreading.

INDEX

Printed in the United States
883500002B